Brilliant Troubleshooting and Repairing your PC

John Taylor

PEARSON
Prentice
Hall

Harlow, England • London • New York • Boston • San Francisco • Toronto • Sydney • Singapore • Hong Kong
Tokyo • Seoul • Taipei • New Delhi • Cape Town • Madrid • Mexico City • Amsterdam • Munich • Paris • Milan

Pearson Education Limited

Edinburgh Gate

Harlow

Essex CM20 2JE

England

and Associated Companies throughout the world

Visit us on the World Wide Web at:

www.pearsoned.co.uk

First published 2006

ISBN-13: 978-0-13-173398-5

ISBN-10: 0-13-173398-2

British Library Cataloguing-in-Publication Data

A catalogue record for this book is available from the British Library

Library of Congress Cataloging-in-Publication Data

A CIP catalog record for this book can be obtained from the Library of Congress

10 9 8 7 6 5 4 3 2 1

10 09 08 07 06

Prepared for Pearson Education Ltd by Syllaba Ltd (http://www.syllaba.co.uk)

Editorial management by McNidder & Grace, Alnwick

Typeset in Helvetica LT Narrow 11pt by P.K. McBride, Southampton

Printed and bound in Great Britain by Ashford Colour Press Ltd., Gosport.

The publisher's policy is to use paper manufactured from sustainable forests.

Brilliant guides

What you need to know and how to do it

When you're working on your PC and come up against a problem that you're unsure how to solve, or want to accomplish something in an application that you aren't sure how to do, where do you look? Manuals and traditional training guides are usually too big and un-wieldy and are intended to be used as end-to-end training resources, making it hard to get to the info you need right away without having to wade through pages of background information that you just don't need at that moment – and helplines are rarely that helpful!

Brilliant guides have been developed to allow you to find the info you need easily and without fuss and guide you through the task using a highly visual, step-by-step approach – providing exactly what you need to know when you need it!

Brilliant guides provide the quick easy-to-access information that you need, using a de-tailed index and troubleshooting guide to help you find exactly what you need to know, and then presenting each task in a visual manner. Numbered steps guide you through each task or problem, using numerous screenshots to illustrate each step. Added features include 'See also...' boxes that point you to related tasks and information in the book, while 'Did you know?...' sections alert you to relevant expert tips, tricks and advice to further expand your skills and knowledge.

In addition to covering all major office PC applications, and related computing subjects, the *Brilliant* series also contains titles that will help you in every aspect of your working life, such as writing the perfect CV, answering the toughest interview questions and moving on in your career.

Brilliant guides are the light at the end of the tunnel when you are faced with any minor or major task.

Publisher's acknowledgements

The author and publisher would like to thank the following for permission to reproduce the material in this book:

Computing.Net LLC, Creative Element, Google Inc., Kaspersky Lab, Lavasoft, McAfee, Inc., Panda Software, PC Pitstop LLC, Softwin SRL, Symantec Corporation, Trend Micro Incorporated, The WildList Organization International.

Microsoft product screen shot(s) reprinted with permission from Microsoft Corporation.

Every effort has been made to obtain necessary permission with reference to copyright material. The publisher apologises if, inadvertently, any sources remain unacknowledged and will be glad to make the necessary arrangements at the earliest opportunity.

Dedication

I would like to dedicate this book to my wife, Karen, who put up with me getting up at five o'clock every day to start work. Also, to Vince who read every word and corrected my English! And finally to my dog, Charlie, who died just as I was finishing off this book. He was my best friend and I will miss him very much.

About the author

John Taylor has 20 years experience of dealing with computer problems and has been writing about computers for the same amount of time. He has been the editor of many computing magazines, including *Which PC*, *Practical PC*, *Windows Made Easy*, *PC Basics*, *PC Home* and his new launch *DVD Easy*. He has written, edited and compiled over 20 books. When he's not writing, John enjoys horse riding, show jumping and spending time with his pets: four horses, two cats, a dog and a parrot.

Contents

Introduction

Welcome to *Brilliant Troubleshooting & Repairing your PC*, a visual quick reference book that shows you how to maintain your computer, understand how hardware and software interact, find and fix common problems and secure yourself against potential disasters and crashes.

Find what you need to know – when you need it

You don't have to read this book in any particular order. We've designed the book so that you can jump in, get the information you need, and jump out. To find the information that you need, just look up the task in the table of contents, index, or trouble-shooting guide, and turn to the page listed. Read the task introduction, follow the step-by-step instructions along with the illustration, and you're done.

How this book works

Each task is presented with step-by-step instructions in one column and screen illustrations in the other. This arrangement lets you focus on a single task without having to turn the pages too often.

How you'll learn

Find what you need to know – when you need it

How this book works

Step-by-step instructions

Troubleshooting guide

Spelling

Step-by-step instructions

This book provides concise step-by-step instructions that show you how to accomplish a task. Each set of instructions includes illustrations that directly correspond to the easy-to-read steps. Eye-catching text features provide additional helpful information in bite-sized chunks to help you work more efficiently or to teach you more in-depth information. The 'For your information' feature provides tips and techniques to help you work smarter, while the 'See also' cross-references lead you to other parts of the book containing related information about the task. Essential information is highlighted in 'Important' boxes that will ensure you don't miss any vital suggestions and advice.

Troubleshooting guide

This book offers quick and easy ways to diagnose and solve common problems that you might encounter using the Troubleshooting guide. The problems are grouped into categories that are presented alphabetically.

Spelling

You will notice that we have used American spelling conventions throughout this book. We do regret having to do this in a book aimed at UK and Irish readers. However, nearly all the software that we illustrate (Microsoft's being the most prevalent) is written by American developers and in order to be consistent with the spelling you will actually encounter whilst using your PC, we have conformed. Please rest assured that our grammatical conscience struggles as much as yours does with disk, color and program!

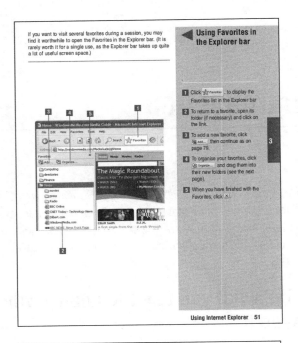

Basic problems explained

Introduction

In this book, we will give you enough knowledge to fix the most commonly encountered problems with a PC but, rest assured, not enough knowledge to do any damage. We assume that you are working with a PC running Windows XP. Windows XP is now a stable platform and does not break easily.

Most problems you might have are software related and can be fixed. With a little forward planning you can save yourself a lot of hassle later. We are going to show you what steps to take to do this.

The main reason for a PC to start playing up is change – computers are like people, and they hate change. Changes come in many forms. Adding a new piece of hardware, installing software applications, downloading (accidentally of course) viruses and spyware – all have one thing in common, they change your PC and its setup. So if you want a stable system don't change anything! However, in the real world change is inevitable. You don't have to be afraid of making changes but you do need to be prepared for the problems they might cause.

A much less frequent problem is hardware failure. It happens, PC parts fail and they can fail at any time. Your PC could work diligently away for many years or fail in its first week. Sometimes a little maintenance is all that is needed to get the hardware working again. Sometimes a more drastic solution like replacing the hardware is in order. Once again you need to be prepared and that means protecting you and your data. In Chapter 4 we will guide you through the process of backing up your data so that a hardware failure need not be catastrophic. This book will help you avoid the traps and the pitfalls and give you a solid strategy which will ensure you can fix most common problems.

What you'll do

Learn about your PC's built-in defences

Use your PC's built-in troubleshooting resources

Diagnose common hardware problems

Identify hardware problems using Device Manager

Diagnose common software problems

Learning about your PC's built-in defences

Many prospective DIY PC troubleshooters are put off ever starting because they think it's far easier to do permanent damage to their PC than it really is. Windows XP has plenty of built-in defences to stop you rashly wrecking your PC. So as long as you are careful and read everything that appears on the screen you should have no problems.

Can you permanently break your PC – No!

It is very difficult to permanently break your PC, you can mess-up the software and give yourself a lot of trouble, but you can't break the hardware by using a mouse or typing anything in via the keyboard. However, you can stop hardware working by ignoring Windows advice and installing non-approved hardware.

Windows XP defences

Windows has many built-in defences; most things you do are not permanent, and if they are, you can always start from scratch and restore the whole system. What's more, Windows will always inform you what you are doing and it will also give you a chance to back out.

- Windows always asks you to confirm drastic actions; for example, if you want to delete a file Windows will display a dialogue box asking if you are sure you want to send the file to the Recycle Bin.

- The Recycle Bin is your next safety net. A deleted file is not really deleted and can be rescued.

Jargon buster

Recycle Bin – a folder linked to an icon on the Windows Desktop where you can drag folders or files that you want to delete. When you put items into the Recycle Bin, they are not permanently deleted, and can be easily recovered by double-clicking on the Bin icon, and restoring them back to their original folders. To permanently delete a file, you need to empty the Bin.

If you want to install a piece of kit that Windows thinks will not work with your system it will ask if you want to go ahead and will explain the consequences of your actions.

Important

Pop-up dialogue boxes are there to be read. Ignore them at your peril!

If you insist on doing something Windows does not recommend, then it will create a restore point. A restore point is a snapshot of your system taken before any potential problem.

Windows will not let you delete any files it is currently using or most system files, thus making it difficult for you to delete vital files.

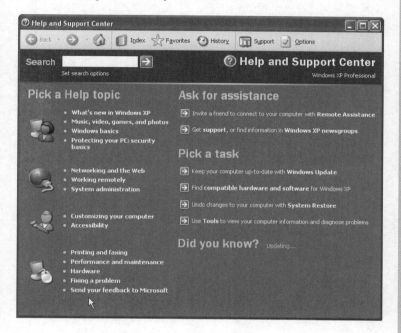

See also

You can find out how to create system restore points before you install any software you are unsure of, in 'Using System Restore' (p.44 in Chapter 4).

Learning about your PC's built-in defences (cont.)

1

Using your PC's built-in troubleshooting resources

Use Windows Help

If in doubt make use of Help. It comes in many forms.

Windows Help can be used as a manual and is searchable – which means you should be able to find the answer to your problem quickly. It's great for answering questions such as the 'how do I?' type.

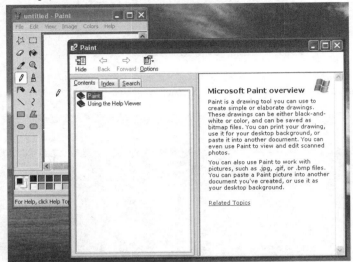

Basic searchable Help can be found in every program. It is always found on the main toolbar on the main screen.

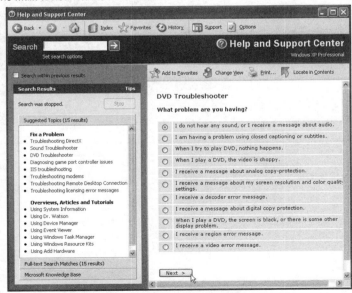

Windows Troubleshooting takes you step-by-step through problems by presenting you with a series of questions, the answers to which guide you to the solution.

Use Microsoft Knowledge Base

It's pretty much guaranteed that someone has experienced the exact same problem as you have. Microsoft documents all this information and makes it available in one massive searchable database.

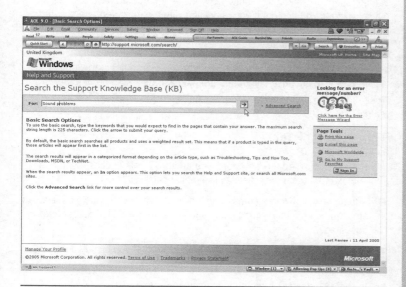

For your information

You can find the Microsoft Knowledge Base at:

http://support.microsoft.com/search

Diagnosing common hardware problems

One of the first things you need to try and find out when your computer has stopped working or started behaving badly, is why. You'll find that the problem is nearly always a software problem. However, the fact that software problems are so common, coupled with our belief that our computer will go on forever, means that we often forget to look at the hardware. It is important, if you don't want to spend too much time barking up the wrong tree, to have a strategy which will help you find out if you're dealing with a hardware or a software problem. Check for hardware problems first. Anything mechanical will sooner or later wear and eventually break.

Generally, when hardware breaks it stays broke; it does not start working again. However, because computers are modular, they are one of the few modern devices that you can buy spare parts for (off the shelf) and fix yourself.

Jargon buster

A **peripheral** is something not core to your computer; this usually means an add-on like a web-cam or speakers. Most peripherals are extra things you buy to add to the functionality of your computer such as a printer or scanner.

Driver – a small program that enables add-on accessories to talk to your computer. Without the appropriate driver software installed, Windows cannot transmit to or receive from a device, whether it's a printer, CD-ROM drive or scanner.

Things to look for

- Have you installed any new hardware add-ons? This applies to internal and external temporary devices like digital cameras?

- Adding new hardware means adding new drivers. Incompatible drivers can stop Windows working completely and Windows will never get past the boot stage.

- Did Windows warn you there might be a problem if you installed this hardware driver?

- Is everything plugged in and is the power turned on?

- Do the lights come on?

- Does the fan wind up?

- Is the computer or device very hot? If it is turn it off and get it fixed.

- Is the monitor turned on and receiving a signal? Many monitors will tell you if they are not connected to the computer either by displaying a message on screen or by turning the power LED light amber. Green is on and OK, amber means no signal.

- Is the brightness and contrast turned up on the monitor? The monitor may look blank if they are turned down. This can usually be adjusted by using the monitors inbuilt menu system or on screen display (OSD), usually activated by pushing the button marked menu.

Important

If a printer stops printing altogether bear in mind that it could be a software related problem – it does not necessarily follow that the printer is broken. A quick test on another computer should show you if the printer is broken or not. Or you can always try reinstalling the software that came with the printer.

6

If a piece of hardware stops working you can check its status with Windows built-in software. The Device Manager provides you with a graphical view of the hardware that is installed on your computer. You can use Device Manager to update the drivers (or software) for hardware devices, modify hardware settings, and troubleshoot problems. Device Manager will flag up problem software with a yellow circle.

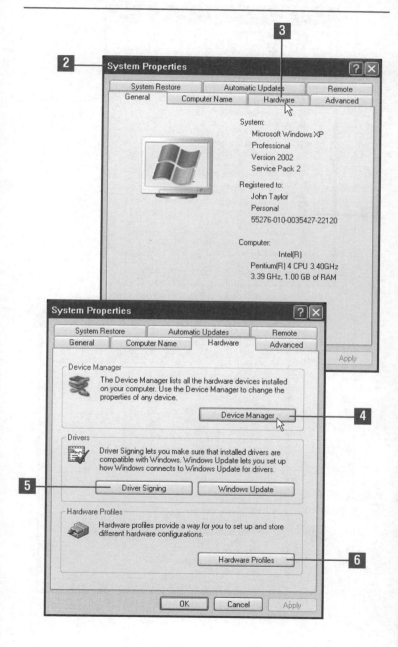

Start Device Manager

1 Open the Start menu and right-click on My Computer to open its context menu. Click on Properties.

2 The System Properties dialog box will now be displayed. There are several tabs at the top of the menu.

3 Click on to the tab marked Hardware.

4 The Hardware tab houses the Device Manager, which is what we need to use to check out the devices connected to the computer system. Click on the Device Manager button.

5 Also on this tab is the Driver control section, this allows you to check that all the drivers currently installed are compatible with Windows. Some may no longer be if you have recently upgraded Windows XP.

6 The Hardware Profiles section allows you to set up your hardware for different uses or situations.

Important

Incorrectly altering your hardware configuration can damage your system. Be sure to read the appropriate instructions before making changes to your hardware configuration.

Identifying hardware problems using Device Manager (cont.)

Use Device Manager

1 The Device Manager menu is now displayed. It is basically a list of all the equipment connected to your computer.

2 If everything is working OK you will just see a list, but if a device has a problem it will be highlighted by a yellow question mark. Click on the plus sign next to the question mark to open up this section of the list.

3 The device with the problem will now be displayed – click the new question mark icon to select it.

Did you know?

Computers themselves can stop. If your PC works OK for a while and then switches off all by itself, it's probably because it's getting too hot. The clue here is that there will be roughly the same period of time between turning on and it switching itself off each time it happens.

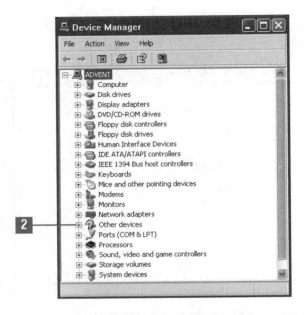

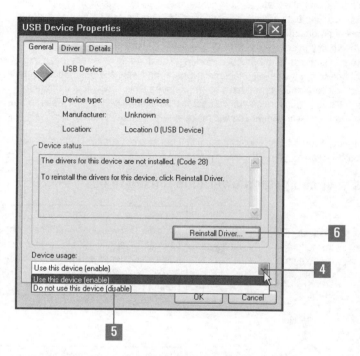

4 The Properties menu for the device is now displayed. Here you can enable or disable the device so that it does not interfere with any other devices. Click on the down arrow to the right of the Device usage box.

5 A drop down list is now displayed. Click on Do not use this device (disable) to disable the device.

6 Alternatively, if a device is not functioning it is often because the driver has not been successfully installed. To reinstall the driver click on the button marked Reinstall Driver.

7 The Hardware Update Wizard will now start. Follow its instructions to reinstall the driver. Make sure you have any driver disks handy.

Jargon buster

Wizard – a special program that provides a step-by-step guide to performing a task, such as installing a printer. It tells you what to do and prompts you to enter any information it requires.

Diagnosing common software problems

Hardware failures are pretty predictable, computers and peripherals either work or they don't. So, if you have eliminated the possibility of hardware failure, it must be your software that's broken. Unfortunately, software can be a little less predictable than hardware. So if a problem occurs somewhat randomly it's probably a software glitch. Software breaks more frequently than hardware because it is used to control everything a computer does. Most software, including Windows itself, has bugs and these only surface in certain combinations of situations. This means that if software is working it should keep working until something changes. This change can be new software being introduced to the computer system or a major upgrade to Windows. When many users upgraded to Windows XP Service Pack 2 some older programs and software stopped working. The good news is that these bugs will nearly always have surfaced elsewhere, and will have been documented, and software updates will have been produced. This is why it is important to register your software so you can get technical support. Regular visits to the software house's home page will make sure you keep up-to-date.

Like the human body, your computer will get slower with age, but unlike the body, we can fix your Windows system!

For your information

You can find the Microsoft Knowledge Base at:

http://support.microsoft.com/search

Is your computer slower than it used to be?

See also

Using the Control Panel (see p.29 in Chapter 3).

See also

Using Disk Clean up (see p.99 in Chapter 9).

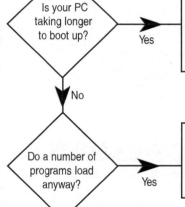

Is your PC taking longer to boot up? — Yes → Remove any programs from your Start Up folder that you don't often use such as Real Player and MS Messenger. You may need to remove the program using Add or Remove Programs in the Control Panel.

No ↓

Do a number of programs load anyway? — Yes → You may have some programs that have installed themselves into the system registry. To solve this, you'll need to use MSConfig to stop them running at startup.

No ↓

Do programs take longer to load? Is the disk very active while they run? — Yes → Are you running low on disk space? Check My Computer to see if you've run out of room. Use the Disk Clean up utility in your system applications folder to remove unwanted files.

No ↓

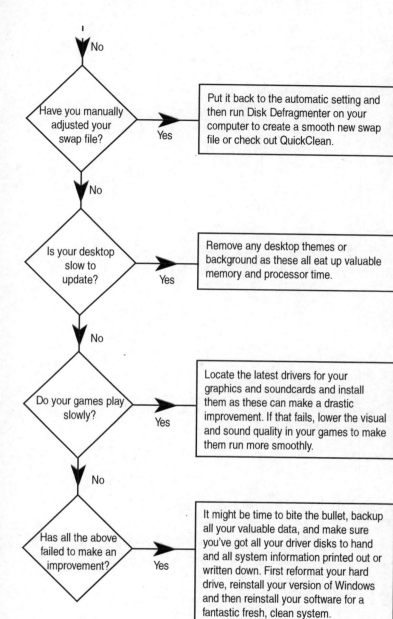

No

Have you manually adjusted your swap file? — Yes → Put it back to the automatic setting and then run Disk Defragmenter on your computer to create a smooth new swap file or check out QuickClean.

No

Is your desktop slow to update? — Yes → Remove any desktop themes or background as these all eat up valuable memory and processor time.

No

Do your games play slowly? — Yes → Locate the latest drivers for your graphics and soundcards and install them as these can make a drastic improvement. If that fails, lower the visual and sound quality in your games to make them run more smoothly.

No

Has all the above failed to make an improvement? — Yes → It might be time to bite the bullet, backup all your valuable data, and make sure you've got all your driver disks to hand and all system information printed out or written down. First reformat your hard drive, reinstall your version of Windows and then reinstall your software for a fantastic fresh, clean system.

See also

Using Disk Defragmenter (see p.102 in Chapter 9).

See also

Backing up (Chapter 4) and Hard drives (Chapter 9 and Chapter 15).

Introducing your PC

2

Introduction

It is reasonably safe to open a computer case – the high voltage is locked away where you can't touch it. So take a look inside. There is only low voltage DC current supplying the components outside the power supply. At first it will look confusing but this chapter will show you what the components do and where they are.

It pays to know what you are looking at when you open your PC, as this helps to demystify what's inside. Many problems can be tracked down to a specific fault. On the rare occasion where the problem lies with hardware, the hardware is usually inside your PC. Over the years, computer layouts have come to be standardised and so once you have learned the basic layout of a computer you should have no trouble identifying bits of hardware regardless of the make and model of your PC. This standardisation in the industry also means you can buy off the shelf additions for your PC. All the components can be replaced, including the whole motherboard, and it's not uncommon for PC upgraders to do this regularly to keep their PC as state-of-the-art as possible.

What you'll do

Learn which parts can be easily replaced or upgraded

Recognise PC connections

Recognise PC components

Learn your way around a motherboard

Recognise the main components on a graphics card

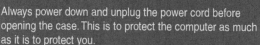

Important

Always power down and unplug the power cord before opening the case. This is to protect the computer as much as it is to protect you.

Learning which parts can be easily replaced or upgraded

The motherboard

The motherboard is the biggest component in a computer system. It is one large printed circuit board, which is the foundation for the rest of the computer. This board is home to various plugs and sockets which make the PC truly modular.

The graphics card or display card

A graphics display card is a mini computer in itself. It has a processor and its own memory. Not all graphics cards are equal. If you are an avid games player you might want to consider one of the specialised games cards. Note that many PCs have their graphics built-in to the motherboard.

The processor (CPU)

Processors are manufactured by two main players; Intel and AMD. The processors are available in ever increasing speeds measured in megahertz (MHz). The processor is located in a socket on the main motherboard. If the processor goes wrong it is a quick job to replace it.

The memory

Memory comes in many different formats. When replacing memory it is better to remove one of the existing memory sticks and take it with you to the shop, as this way you will be assured to get the right format, speed and type of memory.

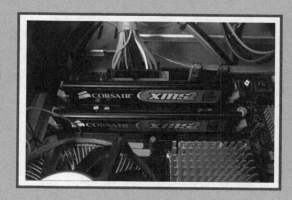

The CD-ROM/DVD drives

CD-ROM/DVD drives have become more powerful and much cheaper in recent years. These drives do go wrong and sometimes need maintenance. These days changing a faulty drive will cost very little and you will get the added advantage of a much faster drive with much more functionality.

The hard drives

Hard drives get taken for granted, they are reliable but they are not indestructible; it's because they are so reliable that we end up trusting them to go on serving us for years. They can go wrong though and when they do it's the most disruptive, most devastating thing that can happen to a computer. You will loose all your data! There are disaster recovery houses that can retrieve data but they are expensive. Better to remember that most important rule in computing – back up your data religiously!

Recognising PC connections

The original concept for the first commercially available PC was used by IBM and most early PCs that followed this design were said to be IBM compatible. This design for a computer was all about standards and these standards made it possible for you to interchange both hardware and software. All PCs today follow the same basic design. This means once you have figured out how one PC is put together you have figured out them all.

Graphics port
The monitor or display device plugs into this port, your monitor has a 15 pin plug which fits into this socket. Nothing else is designed to fit this socket.

Power supply socket
Power supply cords need to be fully plugged in to make contact. All power cords are made to European standards.

Mouse and keyboard ports
The mouse and keyboard ports look the same and it is possible to get the mouse and keyboard the wrong way around. For this reason they are color coded and will have a picture of a mouse or keyboard next to them.

Serial port
This socket was also known as the RS232 interface. Different kinds of devices can plug into a serial port, such as modems and mice. Devices that connect to this port have 9 pins – the computer refers to these ports as COM ports.

Parallel or printer port
This socket used to be the main connection point for printers. Other devices such as scanners also used to connect to this port. The advent of USB ports made this port redundant. Your PC calls this port LPT1 or LPT2.

Universal serial bus (USB)
The USB port supports plug and play installation. Using USB, you can connect and disconnect devices without shutting down or restarting your computer. You can use a single USB port to connect up to 127 peripheral devices, including speakers, telephones, CD-ROM drives, joysticks, tape drives, keyboards, scanners and cameras.

Network connection
Many computers, but not all, have built-in network sockets. This allows connection to a Local Area Network or LAN. Broadband modems and routers also use this socket.

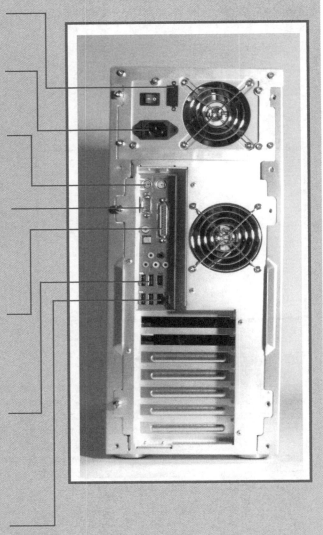

Did you know?

New PCs also have a Firewire fast data transfer port. Firewire is used for any device that needs to transfer large amounts of data making them ideal for external hard drives and connection of video devices such as a video camcorder.

2

Power cooling fan
The power supply is encased in a box; the components generate heat. This heat is removed by circulating air through the box.

Case cooling fan
The main processor and graphics card along with most of the other components also generate heat. The processor and graphics card will have their own fans. Some cases have a second case fan.

Expansion slots
These slots are protected by steel plates. These plates can be removed when an expansion card is fitted.

Did you know?

Many PCs have on-board soundcards. There are several sockets associated with sound. All these sockets are color coded and have pictures of the device that should be plugged into the socket next to them. Typical sockets include speaker outputs, microphone input, line out and surround sound out.

Recognising PC components

Optical drive
CD-ROM, CD-RW, DVD, DVD+R, DVD-R and Dual layer drives. Many drives are now available which can handle all these formats so you don't have to have lots of different drives.

Floppy drive
The floppy drive accepts 3.5-inch disks. These are now all but redundant.

Power switch
The on-off switch, this does not control the power directly. It simply sends a message to the computer to turn it on and off. This eliminates the danger of high voltage. Many PCs will switch off automatically on shut down.

Reset switch
Only used when things go wrong – to restart your computer when it has become frozen.

Indicator light
The power light tells you whether the power is on or off.

The motherboard is the largest component in a computer system. It's a big printed circuit board, which hold the chip sets and support circuitry and expansion slots as well as the main processor socket. Motherboards can also be called system boards.

Learning your way around the motherboard

Expansion slots
Add on cards fit into these slots. There is a specialised slot for the graphics card and some standard slots called peripheral component interconnect (PCI) slots for expansion cards like modems or WiFi cards. These slots are designed to only accept cards that are meant for them. It is impossible to put the wrong card in the wrong slot.

The advanced graphics (AGP) slot
Most new faster graphics cards now use this slot.

Microprocessor (CPU)
The CPU is the brains of the computer. It sits on the motherboard in a socket and the CPU can easily be removed to replace if it goes wrong or if you just want to upgrade to a faster processor.

Memory banks
Most motherboards have several sets of memory sockets or banks. This allows you to add more memory or replace faulty memory. Memory is where programs run, the more memory you have the more programs you can run and the faster your PC will operate.

Jumper switches
These allow you to tailor the motherboard settings. Don't change these unless you have the motherboard manual, as every manufacturers jumper switches are different.

IDE connectors
These allow you to connect hard drives and CD-ROM/DVD drives to the system.

CMOS battery
A small backup battery that provides power to the CMOS chip. The CMOS chip holds information about the configuration of the computer. If this battery is flat the CMOS will loose the information and prevent your PC from working.

Recognising the main components on the graphics card

A graphics card provides specialised graphics acceleration, allowing for advanced visuals and effects. Using a dedicated card rather than an onboard graphics solution takes pressure off the CPU

S Video output socket
Used to connect your PC to your TV or Home cinema system.

Graphics memory
The more memory, the more complicated graphics the card can display.

Digital socket
This is where newer LCD flat panels connect.

VGA socket
This is where the monitor plugs in. This is an older style socket all CRT (old television type) monitors use to connect.

Advanced Graphics (AGP) plug
This fits into the AGP slot on the motherboard.

Important

Never force a component into a slot! If it doesn't fit, it doesn't belong there.

Graphics processor and cooling fan
These chips are run hard and hot – they need a great deal of cooling.

Jargon buster

AGP – an Accelerated Graphics Port is a high speed connection for video cards. On most motherboards there is only one of them and older computers do not have AGP. AGP is faster than PCI and has direct access to system memory so that the computer's memory it is therefore better for 3D graphics and games

Inside Windows XP

Introduction

Windows XP is a complete operating system. It controls and configures all the elements that go to make up your computer from the keyboard to the monitor and everything inside the PC's box. No two computers are completely the same – they might start off that way when they first come out of the box but they quickly change depending on the software installed, the software features used and the peripherals added by the user – you. This means that Windows needs to be highly flexible and for that reason it's very complicated. Once Windows has control of the hardware it needs to give that control to you. It does this through an interface. The main screen of Windows looks remarkably bare. Windows XP is designed this way, to look and feel simple to use.

What you'll do

Explore the Windows XP desktop

Navigate the desktop

Find out where Windows came from

Customise the Taskbar

Find out which version of Windows XP you have

Use Automatic Updates

Explore the Control Panel

Finding out where Windows came from

In November 1983 Microsoft, makers of the MSDOS operating system, announced Microsoft Windows; an extension of the MSDOS system. Windows was Microsoft's first Graphical User Interface (GUI). The evolution of computers from text-based instruction systems to icon-based control had begun.

Windows through time

1990 Windows 3x

1993 Windows NT

1995 Windows 95

1996 Windows NT workstation

1998 Windows 98

2000 Windows Me and Windows 2000

2001 Windows XP Home and Windows XP professional

2006 Windows Vista launch due October

Exploring the Windows XP desktop

Windows XP is an interface made of menus and icons. The desktop is just like a real desktop. Unlike your real desk it has wallpaper and you can change that wallpaper to customise the way Windows looks. Windows starts out with a desktop called Bliss. Bliss is rolling hills and a summer sky. At first sight it seems that there is hardly anything to work with. Let's get past the first screen.

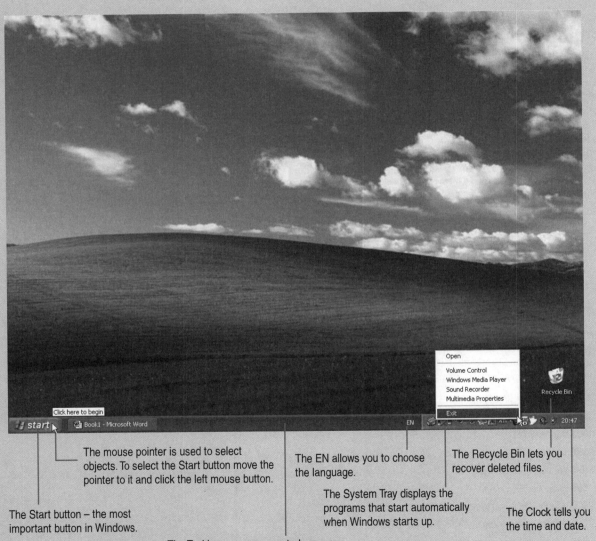

The mouse pointer is used to select objects. To select the Start button move the pointer to it and click the left mouse button.

The EN allows you to choose the language.

The Recycle Bin lets you recover deleted files.

The System Tray displays the programs that start automatically when Windows starts up.

The Start button – the most important button in Windows.

The Clock tells you the time and date.

The Taskbar – you can control programs from here and switch between then.

22

Best practice is to keep the main Windows area, the desktop, clear. It is all too easy to clutter it up with shortcuts documents and pictures. Don't do it. If something goes wrong with the drive that contains Windows and the desktop, then you will lose everything on the desktop. Always save documents and pictures to separate folders, preferably on a different data hard drive.

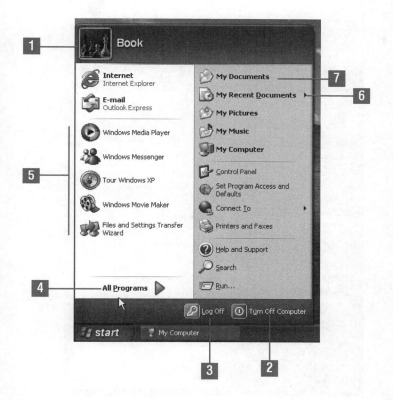

1 After you have clicked on the Start button a pop-up menu is displayed. This Start menu is a vital part of Windows, containing links to applications and various parts of the system such as the Control Panel.

2 Here you can turn off the computer.

3 Log off the computer to change user accounts.

4 Select and run a program.

5 Quickly run a program you have recently run.

6 Open a recent document.

7 Open a document, picture or music file.

Did you know?

You can click the right mouse button on any of the icons in the System Tray and a context menu will be displayed. Many of the programs will have an exit option. You can use this to stop the program and free up some memory. This is useful if your PC is running slowly.

Jargon buster

Context menu – the term given to the menu that appears when you right-click, so called because its functions change depending on the program or area of the operating system in which you currently reside.

System Tray – the little box on the right-hand side of the Taskbar in Windows. As well as displaying the time and date, it is a place where you can quickly launch various system configuration tools, such as the Volume control and, if you have one installed, a Virus scanner. The System Tray is also used to display the status of certain Windows functions, such as when you're connected to the internet.

Navigating the desktop (cont.)

1 Every application and utility program runs in its own window. They all have the same set of controls in the top left corner.

2 Clicking on the close box will close the window.

3 The maximise button will make the window full sized (as big as it can go).

4 The minimise button makes the window into a button on the Taskbar at the bottom of the screen.

Did you know?

When you first start Windows XP you will be asked to take a tour. Do! It will fast track you to a basic understanding of Windows XP. If you turn off this feature, it will disappear and be hard to find again. If you do not turn it off you will be asked to take the tour every time you open Windows. So, take the tour as many times as you need to feel you have a basic understanding of Windows XP, then turn it off. It gets annoying being asked every time you open Windows. Just remember once you turn it off, you will never see the invitation to take this hard to find tour again!

Jargon buster

Application – an executable program capable of performing a specialized function, other than system maintenance (which is performed by utilities). Games, educational programs, and communications software are all examples, as are word processors, spreadsheets and databases.

The taskbar is the bar at the bottom of the display in Windows that stretches from one side of the display to the other. Program icons are shown here allowing you to access any application running by clicking it on the Taskbar. You can tell Windows to automatically hide the Taskbar when you're not using it. It will then only pop-up when you move the mouse pointer to the bottom of the screen

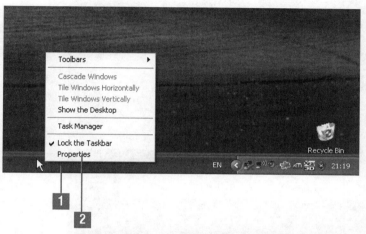

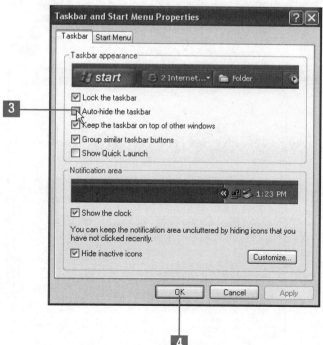

Customising the taskbar

1 Move the mouse pointer to an empty space on the taskbar and click the right mouse button.

2 Click Properties.

3 Click in the box next to Auto-hide the taskbar to place a tick there.

4 Click OK to finish.

3

Jargon buster

Icons – on-screen symbols or pictures that relate to program files or other computer functions. Clicking on an icon will start an action, e.g. open a file or run a program. The picture will usually give a clue as to what the program does or which program a file is used with.

Finding out which version of Windows XP you have

1. Click the Start button to open the Start menu.

2. Right-click on My Computer.

3. Click on Properties.

4. Make sure the General tab is selected by clicking on it.

5. The version of Windows you are currently running is displayed under System.

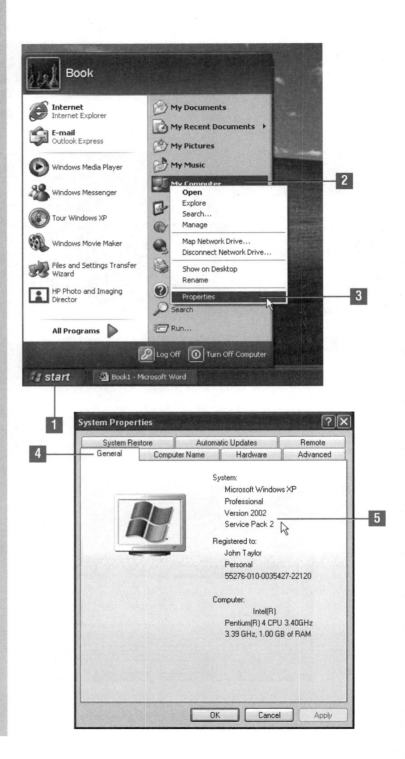

When you turn on Automatic Updates, Windows routinely checks the Windows Update website for high-priority updates that can help protect your computer from the latest viruses and other security threats. These can include security updates, critical updates and service packs. Depending on the setting you choose, Windows will automatically download and install any high-priority updates that your PC needs, or notify you as these updates become available.

The Automatic updates system uses the internet to keep your computer bang up-to-date and therefore safe (or safer). Because this is done automatically you don't have to constantly check to see if a new threat has been discovered.

Using Automatic Updates

1. Click on the Start button, then right-click on My Computer and select Properties.

2. The System Properties menu will now be displayed. Select the Automatic Updates tab.

3. The Automatic Updates menu allows you to switch automatic updates on and off. The default is on. If you don't have internet access you might want to switch this off. To do so click the radio button next to the red shield.

4. You can configure how often the internet is checked for updates. We recommended you leave this set to its default.

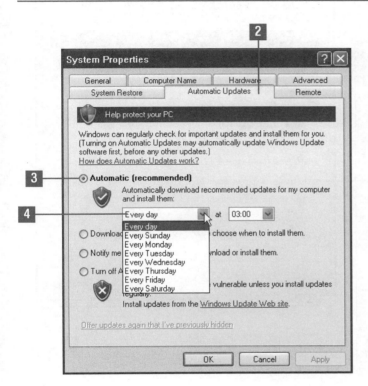

Important

Automatic updates are extremely important to keeping your computer working efficiently. Microsoft not only fixes bugs in the system, but is also fighting a constant war against people who want to make your PC experience a less than happy one.

Jargon buster

Live updates – allow a program to download new versions of itself or, in the case of spyware and antivirus tools, new information about threats to keep your system protected. Generally, live updates should be done in the background without requiring any user intervention.

Using Automatic Updates (cont.)

5 You can choose when the updates are installed. You may want to change this to 'notify me' before downloading and installing. This is because some updates may be incompatible with particular hardware or software – and you need some control.

6 Once you have finished configuring Automatic Updates click on Apply.

See also

'Use GoBack' and 'Use System Restore' (Chapter 4) to effectively uninstall an update that causes problems. They do sometimes destabilise the status quo!

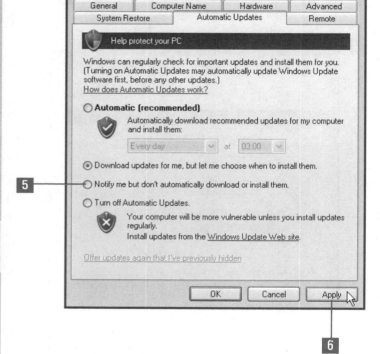

Timesaver tip

Installing updates before you shut down your computer is another way to keep your computer up-to-date and more secure. This option is available only in Microsoft Windows XP with Service Pack 2 (SP2), Microsoft Windows Server 2003 with Service Pack 1 (SP1), or an x64-based version of a Windows Server 2003 or Windows XP operating system and only if important updates have been downloaded but not yet installed. Do not turn off or unplug your computer while updates are installing. Windows will automatically turn off your computer after the updates are installed.

One of the most powerful menus in Windows is the Control Panel. This is because it's packed with tools to customise and control your computer. It should be your first stop if you need to install new hardware, add or remove programs, or change the way your computer looks. The Control Panel has a number of administrative tools, allowing you to control your computer and all its users. It also allows you to customise your computer and change the way it works to suit you. Other tools help you set up Windows and configure add-ons such as modems, printers, mice and scanners. It is important you become familiar with this menu – as the name implies it is the control centre for the whole computer.

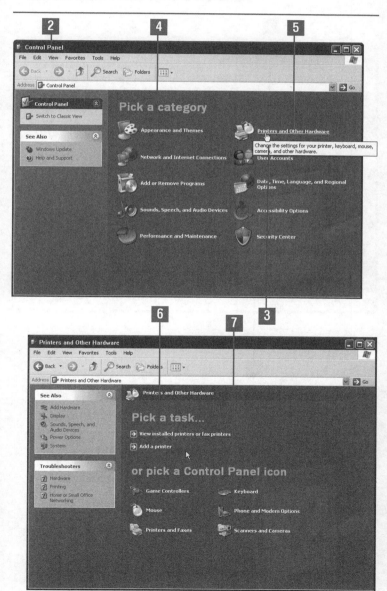

Exploring the Control Panel

Use the Control Panel

1 To open the Control Panel, click Start and then click Control Panel.

2 The Control Panel menu is now displayed. This menu contains 10 sub-categories all of which control your computer in some way. To select a category click on its icon.

3 To find out more information about an item in the Control Panel while in Category view, hold your mouse pointer over the icon or category name and read the text that appears.

4 Some of these items will open to a list of tasks you can perform, as well as a selection of individual Control Panel items. For example, when you click Appearance and Themes, you will see a list of tasks such as Choose a screen saver along with individual Control Panel items.

5 To install or configure your printer click the Printer and other hardware icon. You can also use this menu to configure your mouse and keyboard.

6 Now you are asked to pick a task, e.g. view installed printers or add a new printer.

7 You can also configure six other device types including game controllers, such as joysticks or game pads, keyboards, mice, modems, scanners and cameras.

3

Exploring the Control Panel (cont.)

Remove programs

1 The Add or Remove Programs menu is the place where you remove programs you no longer want.

2 When you click on the icon you will be presented with a long list of every program installed on your computer.

3 Click on the program you want to remove to highlight it.

4 Now click the Change/Remove button to start the uninstaller for that program.

Important

The Add or Remove program is the only safe way to remove programs from your computer. Do not remove them any other way.

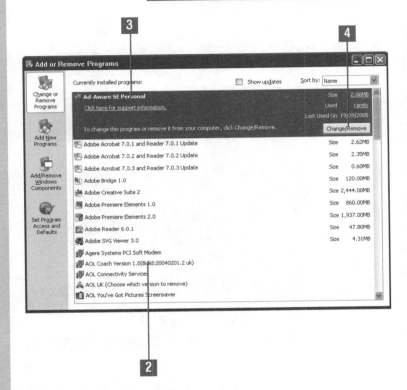

For your Information

If you open Control Panel and do not see the item you want, click Switch to Classic View. If your computer is already set up in Classic View using the more familiar Start menu, click Start, point to Settings, and then click Control Panel. To open an item, double-click its icon.

The Performance and Maintenance menu is probably the most important and most powerful menu in Windows XP and definitely one of the first places you should visit when troubleshooting your computer.

The Security Centre is the place where you configure your computer's security.

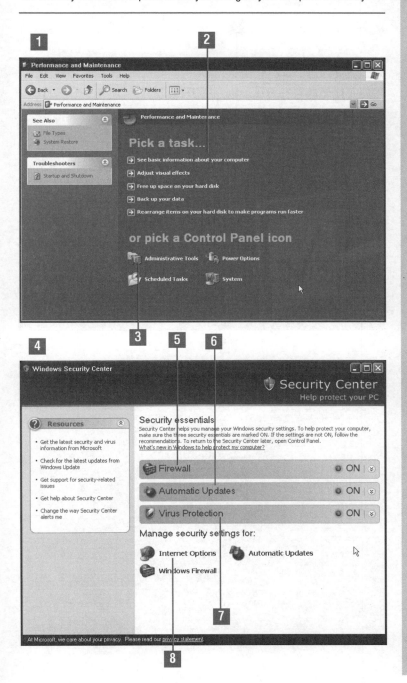

Performance and Maintenance

1 At the Control Panel, select Performance and Maintenance.

2 Here you can pick a task such as looking at the basic information about your computer.

3 You can also go on to do the administration for your PC, schedule tasks and set power options.

Security Center

4 At the Control Panel, select Security Center.

5 You can switch the firewall on and off as well as controlling what it does.

6 You can configure Automatic Updates.

7 If you have virus protection you can control it here.

8 You can also manage internet security.

3

Exploring the Control Panel (cont.)

Sounds, Speech and Audio Devices

1 Here you can control all the sounds and sound devices for your computer.

2 You can control the volume.

3 Change the sound scheme; this can be fun as you can pick new sounds for button clicks and warnings, etc.

4 You can also control any portable devices and work with speech.

Network and Internet Connections

5 The Network and Internet Connections menu controls all your internet settings – most of the configuration is done with the help of wizards that guide you through the tasks.

6 You can also pick an icon to look at specific areas of the internet and network configuration.

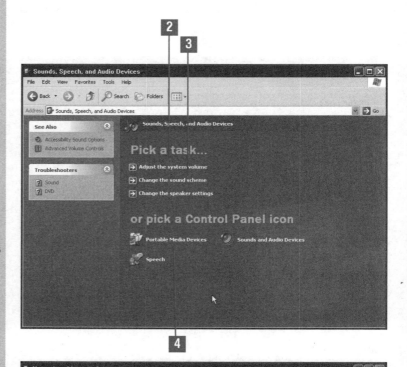

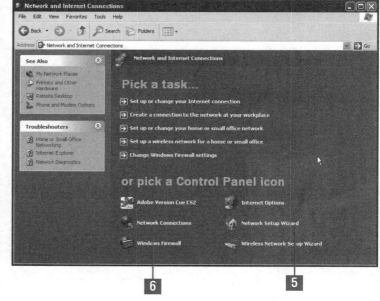

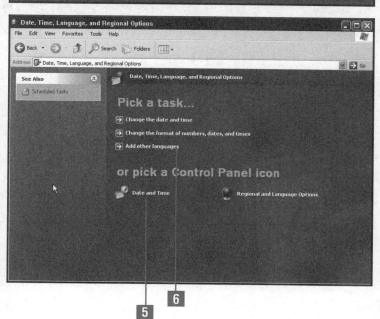

User Accounts

1 Here you can work with user accounts. You can change user's rights – you allow them to have as much control of the computer as you want.

2 You can create a new account.

3 You can also configure the way Windows deals with different users.

3

Date, Time, Language, and Regional options

4 This menu deals with localisation of Windows XP; you can make sure your computer is configured to UK settings.

5 Change the way Windows displays numbers, dates and times.

6 You can add other languages if you use more than one.

Exploring the Control Panel (cont.)

Accessibility Options

1 The Accessibility Options menu is very important as it allows you to adjust settings to suit your vision, hearing and mobility needs.

2 You can change text and icon sizes so that Windows turns into the equivalent of a large print book with everything displayed larger on screen.

3 You can also adjust the mouse and keyboard settings if your mobility is restricted.

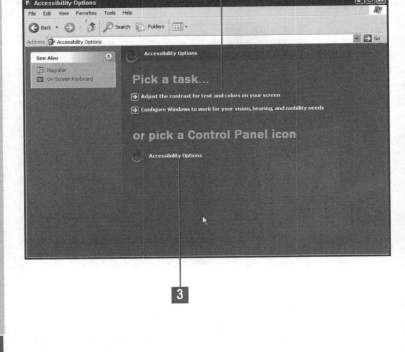

Important

If you need additional help on any Control Panel item, you can find it easily in Help and Support.

Preventing problems

4

Introduction

Regular backups will prevent you losing precious data. Imagine losing all your digital photos for 2004, what a disaster! There was a time when, if a hard drive stopped working, all you would lose was a few documents. Those documents were so small you could back them up by copying them to a bunch of floppy disks. Today, however, PCs have, in many cases, become the central storage point for our entertainment and our memories. This information is too important to trust to one storage device. It needs to be backed up. However, a year's supply of pictures, not to mention two or three home videos, soon takes up a large amount of drive space. We don't realise this until we come to back up the information because today's hard drives are so big. So when it comes to backing up all your data, a floppy has no chance, sometimes not even a CD will do. DVD is the only real option. You can back up using CDs, just make sure you have a lot of them!

In the next section we are going to use Microsoft's own backup utility. This came with all versions of Windows, through to Windows 98 and is still installed with Windows XP Professional. However, if you use Windows XP Home the backup utility is hidden away on the installation CD, and you will have to install it.

What you'll do

Backup your data

Find the Backup program

Use System Restore

Create a restore point

Use GoBack, a commercial program

Use GoBack to revert a drive to an earlier time

Revert your hard disk from the GoBack Boot menu

Learn about online backup services

Backing up your data

The Backup utility helps you protect data from accidental loss if your computer has a hardware or storage media failure. For example, you can use Backup to create a duplicate copy of the data on your hard disk and then archive the data on another storage device. The backup storage medium can be a logical drive such as your hard drive, or a separate storage device such as a removable disk, or an entire library of disks or tapes organised into a media pool and controlled by a robotic changer. If the original data on your hard disk is accidentally erased or overwritten, or becomes inaccessible because of a hard disk malfunction, you can easily restore the data from the archived copy.

Start Backup

1 Open the Start menu, select All Programs, then Accessories. When its menu appears, point to System Tools and select Backup.

2 Backup will start in Wizard Mode. In this task we are going the use the Advanced Mode. The reason we are doing this is because it's not likely that you have a tape backup device or a vast pile of floppies. So we are using Advanced Mode to give us a little more choice.

3 Click on the Advanced Mode link.

Jargon buster

Archive – a collection of files held for backup purposes.

Backup – a single file containing data that might normally be stored in many files or folders. It is created to safeguard against future data loss due to system failure or overwriting of data.

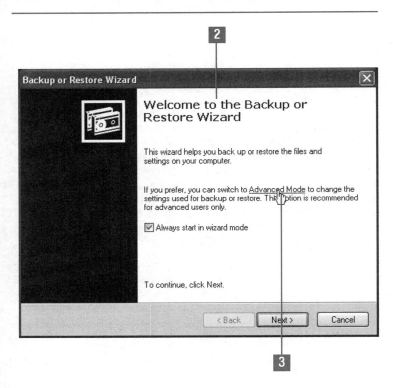

1 The Backup utility window is now displayed. From here you can backup, restore and manage media or schedule future jobs.

2 Select the Backup Wizard (Advanced).

3 You could also use the Restore Wizard (Advanced).

4 The Automated System Recovery Wizard will take you through the procedure to make a full system recovery toolkit.

5 The Backup Wizard is now displayed. Click Next.

Deciding what to backup and where

1. You now need to decide what you want to backup. If this is your first backup then backing up everything on your computer is a good idea.

2. If you have a set of important data files or just a file you can do a selected backup, which will be much quicker. This is a good idea if you are working on files that change over time.

3. The last option lets you backup just the system data. This is a good idea as system files can be corrupted. The registry can have invalid entries which will stop your computer booting. A backup will allow you to replace these files with files that work.

4. In this task, select Backup everything on this computer. Then click Next.

5. Next you need to select where you are going to store your backup file. Click the down arrow to the left of the Browse button. A drop-down box will appear.

6. Select the device you are going to use.

7. Click Next.

For your information

Make sure there is enough storage space on the selected device for your backup. You can make backups that span several disks.

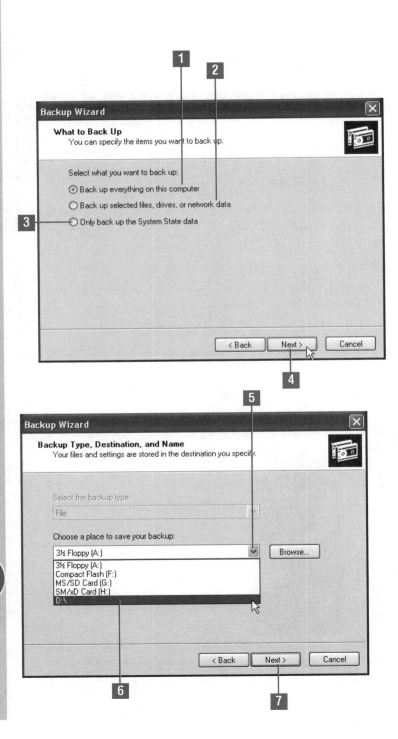

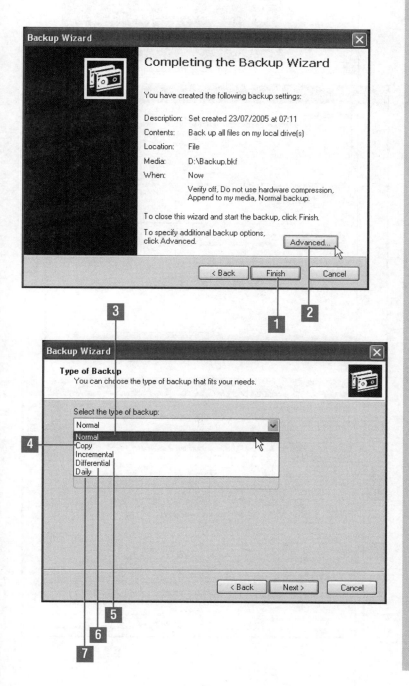

1 At this point you have given Backup most of the information it needs to create a backup. You could click Finish to complete the backup.

2 However, for this task you need to click Advanced.

3 Now you can choose the type of backup you require. Normal is the selection you need for this task. Click Normal then click Next.

4 Selecting Copy makes a copy of an existing backup giving you two identical backup files.

5 Choosing Incremental makes a sequentially numbered backup. This is useful for keeping a trail or restoring an older version of a file while still having the most up-to-date backup.

6 A Differential backup copies files created or changed since the last normal or incremental backup. It does not mark files as having been backed up (in other words, the archive attribute is not cleared). If you are performing a combination of normal and differential backups, restoring files and folders requires that you have the last normal as well as the last differential backup.

7 A Daily backup copies all selected files that have been modified the day the daily backup is performed. The backed up files are not marked as having been backed up (i.e. the archive attribute is not cleared).

Using Backup options

▶

1 Backup Wizard will now ask you to select what options you want to use. The Verify data option takes much longer, but we highly recommend it

2 The second option will be greyed out unless you have a hardware tape device with compression built-in.

3 Windows XP allows you to create shadow copy backups of volumes, exact point-in-time copies of files, including all open files. For example, databases that are held open exclusively and files that are open due to operator or system activity are backed up during a volume shadow copy backup. In this way, files that have changed during the backup window are copied correctly.

4 When you have selected your options, click Next.

5 The next step is to choose whether the Backup will replace any existing backup. This is useful if you are short on space or you are sure you have finished with the old backup. To use this option, select Replace.

6 The safer option is Append to existing backups. This simply changes files that have changed since the last backup.

7 The last option only applies if you have more than one person using the PC. If you have, you can choose to restrict who has access to the backup.

8 When you have selected your options, click Next.

Important

Your backup will be useless if the media you use has errors. Verify is the only certain way of finding out that your data is safe.

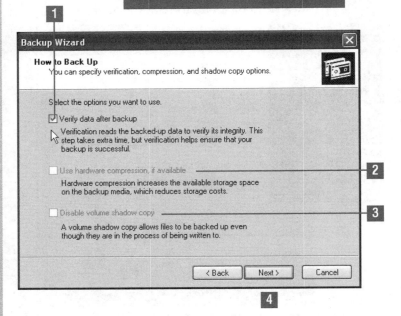

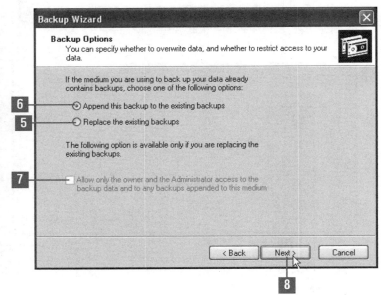

Backup Wizard will now ask you when you want to backup as you can run the backup now or later. The reason these options are here is because backups can take a very long time.

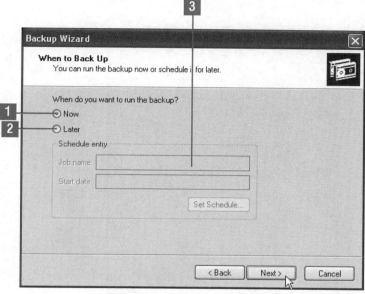

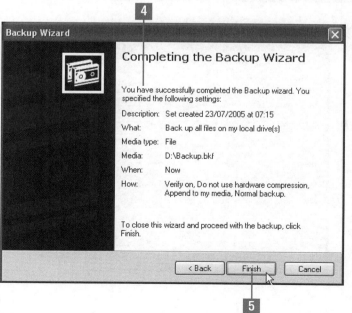

When to backup?

1 If you are happy to start the backup immediately then select the Now radio button.

2 You may wish to carry on using your computer. If you do, select the Later radio button.

3 The Schedule entry box will now be enabled and you will be able to specify the date and time for your backup. Set a time when you know you won't be using your computer. Overnight backups are a good idea.

4 Backup Wizard now displays a summary, listing what, where, when and how the backup will be processed.

5 To start the backup click Finish.

4

Using Backup
options (cont.)

Follow the progress

1 The backup will start; you can cancel the operation at any time by clicking on the Cancel button.

2 Drive and File details are displayed in this section.

3 Progress is displayed with a progress bar but as the backup can take a long time, an elapsed time and an estimated time is also displayed, which is much more useful.

4 This section gives details on exactly what's going on right now. Which file is being processed, how many have been processed, how many will be processed and exactly how many bytes have been processed.

5 Once the backup is complete a report menu is displayed.

6 At this point you can simply click Close to close this box and the backup is complete.

7 If you want a record of the backup select the Report button and a detailed report will be generated.

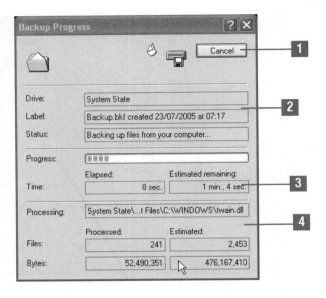

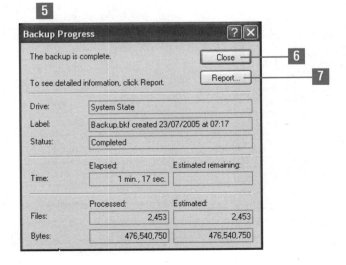

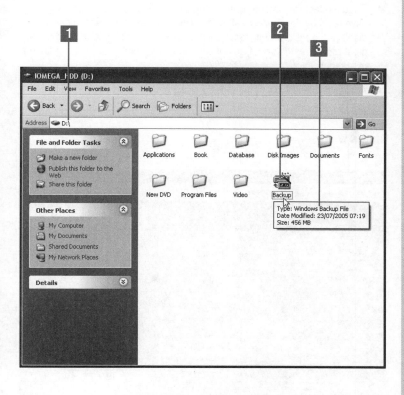

Find your backup

1 The backup file will be found where you specified in the Wizard.

2 Your backup file is easily identified as it has a distinct icon.

3 If you move the mouse pointer over the icon, brief details of the backup are displayed.

4

Find the Backup program

Backup is installed in Windows 2000 and Windows XP Pro and can be found in the System tools menu, off the Accessories section of the Programs menu, off the Start button.

In other versions of Windows, Backup is an extra component. You will have to install it yourself.

Windows 98: To install it in Windows 98 open the Control Panel. Select the Add/Remove icon and double click the mouse button. Now click the left mouse button on the Windows Setup tab. Next, double click System tools and select Backup, click in the box to place a tick.

Windows ME: Backup can be found on the installation CD in the Addons\Msbackup folder. Double click the mouse button on MSBEXP.EXE to install.

Windows XP Home: Backup can be found on the installation CD in the Valueadd\MSFT\ntbackup folder. To install double click the mouse button on the file called NTBACKUP.MSI.

Using System Restore ▶

1 The simplest way of starting System Restore is through the Help and Support Center. Click the Start button then select the Help and Support.

2 The Help and Support Center can guide you through many tasks. Click the System Restore link.

You can use System Restore to perform the following tasks:

■ Start the process of restoring your system by selecting Restore my computer to an earlier time.

■ Create a restore point by selecting Create a Restore Point.

■ Undo the last restoration by selecting Undo my last restoration. If you have recently done a restoration, the Undo my last restoration option is displayed in the System Restore list. You can use this option to undo your most recent restoration. This option is available only after you have done a restoration.

■ Access System Restore settings by clicking on System Restore settings.

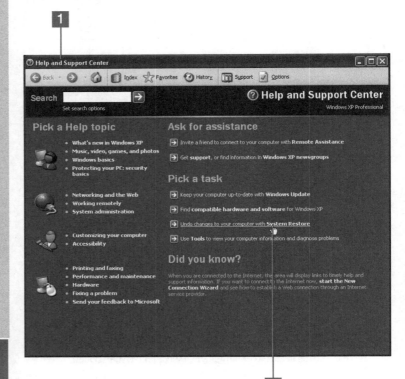

? Did you know?

When you install hardware Windows will automatically set a new restore point, enabling you to revert to a point before you installed the hardware. Windows will also create regular restore points before some programs are installed.

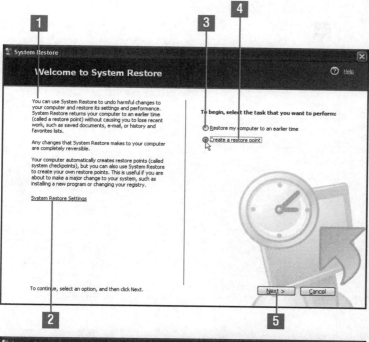

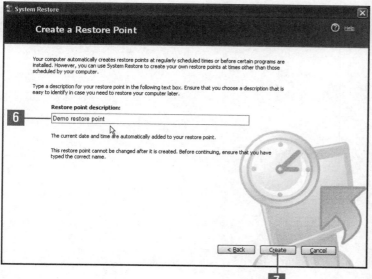

1 When System Restore starts you are given a brief explanation of what System Restore can do.

2 Here you can set System Restore settings. However, we recommend you leave these default settings alone.

3 To restore your computer to an earlier time click on this radio button to select.

4 For this task you need to click on Create a restore point.

5 Click Next.

6 It helps to know why you created a restore point, as there will be several restore points to choose from later. Select the restore point text box and type in your description.

7 When you are done click Create.

4

Using System Restore (cont.)

▶

8 System Restore now displays when your restore point was created.

9 To finish click Home.

For your information

Antivirus utilities can affect whether your system can be restored to a previous point. If a restore point contains an infected file because the utility is not set to clean the file within the restore point, or if an infected file has been removed from a restore point by an antivirus utility because it could not be cleaned, System Restore will not recover the computer to this partial or infected state. If System Restore could not restore your computer to a previous state, and you suspect that one or more restore points contain infected files or have had infected files removed by the antivirus utility, you can remove all restore points from the System Restore archive by turning off System Restore and then turning it back on.

8

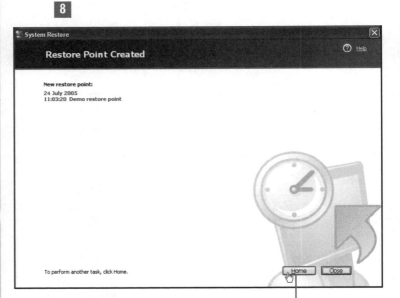

9

There are three primary reasons why you would revert your entire hard disk to an earlier time.

- First, you may have installed new software or made some modification so that your PC no longer works properly (e.g. it will not boot). Perhaps you added hardware, following the instructions to add the device drivers, but something went wrong. Although you can physically remove the new hardware, you need to 'undo' the system changes to get back to where you were.

- Second, your PC is working, but you would like to undo a recent change to the system and you do not know which files to restore. Perhaps you started to print an email, and deleted it, only to find that the printer was out of ink. Ordinarily, the email would be gone. However, with GoBack you can revert your hard disk to before you deleted the email and it will be back.

- Third, you received a virus in an email that infected your hard disk. Again, normally this could mean hours tracking down the infected files, but with GoBack, you can revert your hard disk to a time before you received the email and make your system virus-free again. There are even ways, in the Deluxe Edition's File Rescue feature, to retrieve files that you changed after the virus infected your system.

The common thread in these examples is that you really do not know what specific data to restore in order to back out of a problem. Or even if you do, it is often faster and easier to revert everything to some time in the past.

View your hard disk as it was in the past

You would do this to retrieve an entire folder or look at a set of interdependent files. This is done by creating a virtual GoBack Drive, whose contents correspond to your real hard disk as it was at some time in the past. For example, if C: is your hard disk, then you might ask GoBack to create a virtual GoBack Drive corresponding to C: as it was an hour ago. The virtual GoBack Drive will automatically be assigned a drive letter (for example, D:). This drive D: is very much like a backup of your entire hard disk drive that was made an hour ago. You access drive D: in the same way you would floppy disk A: While you are maintaining a virtual GoBack Drive the system must spend a certain extra effort to keep it up-to-date. Thus, when you are done using your virtual GoBack Drive, you should ask GoBack to discard it.

Retrieving specific files from the past

You can choose to retrieve specific files. For those times when you don't want to completely revert your hard disk just to get back one deleted or overwritten file, you can use the File Recovery Window or the GoBack shell extension in Windows Explorer. Here you can select from various versions of a file by name and date, and either restore it or just bring it back for quick viewing.

Using GoBack, a commercial program

For your information

Deluxe Edition users have extra facilities. After completing the revert hard drive option and logging back into Windows, they are automatically presented with a screen that lets them rescue files that were changed or deleted after the time at which they reverted the drive. Users have the final say on which files they may want to keep.

4

Using GoBack to revert a drive to an earlier time

GoBack integrates itself into the operating system to protect you from data loss. This includes software installation and other problems, deleted or overwritten files, virus attacks, and even system crashes. With GoBack installed, you can back out of trouble, regardless of whether the problem was caused by you, or by software on your machine. Even if your system crashes and will not boot to Windows, you can still recover your system's data. When it is enabled, GoBack keeps track of every event that affects your hard disk. This allows you to retrieve specific files or entirely restore your hard disk.

GoBack is not a backup product because, unlike backup products, GoBack does not involve copying data to a separate tape or disk. Thus, you do not need to stop and make a backup in order to reclaim data created at a certain time in the past. More importantly, you can restore to any point in time, not just to the time at which you created a backup.

1. Buy your copy of Norton GoBack from Symantec at www.symantec.com/goback/

2. Once GoBack is installed, each time you start your computer the GoBack Boot screen appears before the operating system screen displays. You are given several seconds to press the spacebar. If you do not press it, the computer starts normally.

3. If you press the space bar the GoBack Boot menu is displayed.

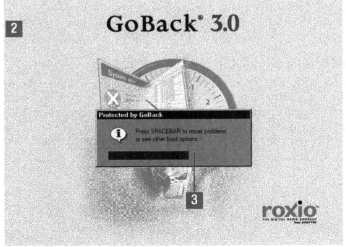

For your information

If your system fails to boot and you are unable to run Windows, use the GoBack Boot menu to perform an emergency recovery – reverting your hard disk back to a time when Windows was operating. When you choose to revert from the GoBack Boot screen, GoBack recommends revert times starting with recent safe points. Choose a point that corresponds to a time when your computer was working fine. If you are not successful the first time you revert, revert again and select a different time. Generally, the first one or two revert attempts will succeed in letting your computer's operating system start again.

If GoBack is not able to revert to a time that allows you to properly start your computer, then you need to restore from your traditional backups. Keep in mind that a physical malfunction – like the microprocessor failing – will not be fixed by either GoBack or a traditional backup, however the data on your hard disk may not be lost either.

4 Revert Drive activates the emergency recovery option. Use this when your PC is unable to boot up normally.

5 Disable GoBack can be used if the operating system is not supported by GoBack and you wish to view all files across all drives, or if you want to use disk-partitioning software. For more information, see Disabling GoBack.

6 Disable/Enable Auto-Revert (Deluxe Edition) is useful if you are testing lots of different software packages, say from a magazine cover disk. Auto-Revert will reset the computer to the point when it was last started thus removing all changes and programs.

7 Boot from floppy is necessary only if you want to boot and run an application from a floppy and have access to your GoBack-protected hard disk(s). For more information, see Booting from a Floppy Disk.

8 Click Continue to proceed with the normal boot process of your system.

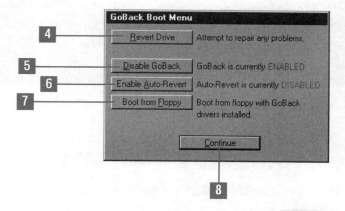

4 — GoBack Boot Menu — Revert Drive — Attempt to repair any problems.

5 — Disable GoBack — GoBack is currently ENABLED

6 — Enable Auto-Revert — Auto-Revert is currently DISABLED

7 — Boot from Floppy — Boot from floppy with GoBack drivers installed.

Continue

8

Important

If it appears that your computer has a physical hardware failure then it should be serviced before you attempt any data recovery. Repeated attempts to recover using GoBack will use up your GoBack history and may reduce the possibility of reverting your hard disk after the physical problems have been repaired.

If you have more than one hard disk protected by GoBack, the revert will affect all these disks.

4

Reverting your hard disk from the GoBack Boot menu

Safe points

1 From the GoBack Boot menu, click Revert Drive. GoBack will search your physical hard disk for safe times (when your hard disk was idle) to which to revert.

2 GoBack identifies safe points and displays them in a dialog box.

3 You can select a time and click Revert.

4 Click More Times to see information about other possible times.

5 Or click Cancel to cancel the revert request.

After you have selected a revert time, and pressed Revert, your system will restart and try to boot. (Remember; do not press the spacebar the second time through the boot process.)

6 If your computer still does not start correctly, repeat Steps 1 to 4 and select a different time.

For your information

After your computer is able to start Windows, you can generally use the GoBack Drive window to select a different time to which to revert your hard disk. The additional information provided in this window may be helpful in selecting a more desirable time.

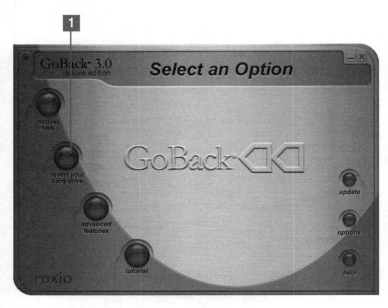

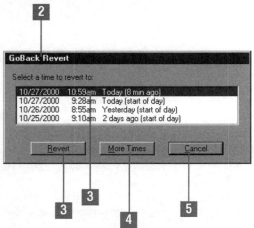

When you think of backing up data, floppy disk, CDs and tape drives are the first thing you probably think of. Before Broadband it was unthinkable to transfer large amounts of data using a slow dial-up connection, but with the advent of easy broadband access, online backup services have become a reliable alternative. In choosing a service, you do have to consider such criteria as speeds and scheduling capabilities, since you'll be transferring large amounts of data over your internet connection. You also want assurances that the company supplying the back up service and your data will be around when you need it. Some companies offer limited free storage for life but many charge a reasonable amount to keep your data safe.

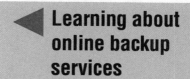

Learning about online backup services

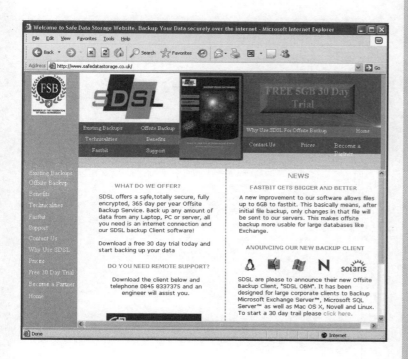

For your information

Safe Data Storage is one of many firms offering online backup – a very inexpensive way to protect your valuable data. Visit them at www.safedatastorage.co.uk or explore the competition by going to Google and running a search for 'online backup'.

4

Dealing with crashes

5

Introduction

There are plenty of things that can go wrong even if your computer isn't completely dead. Your computer can 'crash' at any point which can result in a loss of work, especially if you don't save your work on a regular basis

The big challenge is to pin down the cause and exact nature of the crash. PCs have a nasty habit of never crashing in the same way twice! This doesn't mean that there is more than one thing wrong with them! It's just that they are such complicated devices that the same problem can cause a range of different behaviours depending on exactly what you have been doing.

Perhaps the most frustrating problem of all is the 'big freeze'. This is sometimes referred to as a 'lock-up'. What happens is that you are happily typing away on your machine and it suddenly stops. What is on the screen remains on the screen but using the mouse or the keyboard has no effect; you have a frozen machine!

Do not panic. Check to see if the mouse is working. If it is then there is good chance the PC is just busy doing something. If you wait for it to finish it should unfreeze. Whatever you do, do not start pressing keys at random on the keyboard or moving and clicking the mouse. Each time you do that you give your machine a new instruction to deal with. Eventually, this will simply fill the machine's buffers and you will hear a beeping sound which signifies that your PC cannot accept any more input – the result is a machine that really is frozen.

Sometimes you can work around a crashed program. By pressing the Alt key and the Tab key together, you can switch between applications. You may be able to continue working on different applications.

What you'll do

Shut down a crashed program

Use Task Manager

Find out what causes a crash

Report problems to Microsoft

Delete temporary files to regain storage space

Get support

?

Did you know?

Originally the term 'crash' was only applied to a hard disk failure, but today it means a general problem that stops your machine working.

Shutting down a crashed program

Your computer can, and generally does, run a number of processes and applications at the same time. When for some reason one of these processes or applications ceases to respond, your PC freezes. By shutting down the process that is not responding you are able to continue to work with other running applications. Windows provides a program called Task Manager which can help unfreeze your PC – providing the problem is with a running application or process. The Task Manager lists all of the applications running on your PC, including ones that were started by Windows. If an application has stopped responding it will be listed as 'Not Responding'. If this is the case you should select it and use the End Task button to stop it running. If there is no such application then try ending tasks that aren't important to you so that you can save any documents that are still open in other applications. If all else fails you will have to restart your machine.

Use Task Manager

1 To start Windows Task Manager press and hold Ctrl, followed by Alt, followed by Del keys on the keyboard, until you are holding down all three. Task Manager will now launch.

2 Click on the Applications tab to see running programs. The task window is divided up into two columns – Task and Status. The status will be Running or Not Responding.

3 Select the application you want to stop.

4 Click the End Task button.

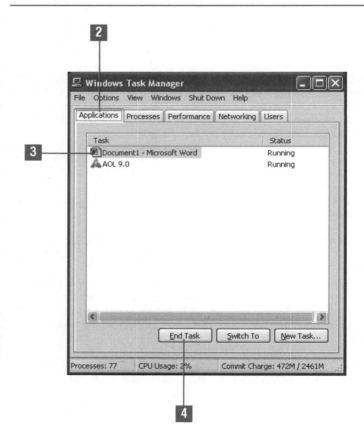

Jargon buster

A **process** is a small program that contains the control information necessary for the execution of a program. If you have an internet connection, firewall and virus protection, the list of processes can be a lengthy one.

If your PC freezes once or twice every few months then you are lucky! Even a perfect PC suffers this fate because it is such a complicated and imperfect machine. These occasional problems are caused by bugs in software. This can include Windows itself and there is nothing you can do about them. However, if your machine is crashing more often than this then there might well be something you can do about it.

How can you tell what it is that causes your PC to crash? The most important indicator is when the crash happens.

- If the PC crashes every time you are using a particular application then the chances are the problem is a bug in that application.

- If the crash tends to happen a set time after you switch your machine on, then you probably have a hardware heat fault. In this case check that the fans on the power supply and processor are actually running. If they aren't then it is time to renew either the entire power supply or the processor fan. You might be able to restart a fan by giving it a push but it will still need to be replaced because it will not be long before it jams again. Even if the fans are running it is worth getting the dust out with a soft paintbrush and see if that cures the problem. To confirm that it is a heat fault try running your PC with the cover open and a domestic fan blowing cold air over it. You can buy cans of freezer compound which you can use to cool individual components to see what is causing the problem, but ask yourself what you are going to do when you narrow the problem down to a single chip! In most cases you will have to take the machine for repair when you have identified a heat fault.

Finding out what causes a crash

For your information

If your machine freezes do not:
1. Press keys randomly.
2. Move the mouse rapidly.
3. Switch off immediately.
4. Hit the PC with something.
5. Unplug and re-plug the keyboard, mouse or monitor.

What you should do is:
1. See if the mouse still moves the cursor. If it does, wait for up to 10 minutes.
2. Try Alt+Tab to switch to another application. If this works save your work and close the application.
3. Try Alt+Ctrl+Del to activate the Task Manager. End any tasks that might be blocking the machine.

If all of this fails then you will have to switch the machine off and on again.

5

Jargon buster

Bug – a malfunction due to an error in the software or a defect in the hardware. Programs don't work as they should, become erratic or stop working.

Reporting problems to Microsoft

When an error occurs, the computer displays an error message. If this error is a system error a blue screen containing error codes is displayed and all computer operations stop. This screen is nicknamed the 'blue screen of death' as you cannot recover from it and your only option is to restart the computer. Illegal operation errors are so called because an application or driver has tried to access or change protected system files or perform a function outside the capability of the machine. Program errors generally affect only the application you are running at the time, giving you a chance to end the program without having to restart your computer.

1 To configure error reporting, first click on the Start button and select Control Panel.

2 Select the Performance and Maintenance category.

3 Click the System icon.

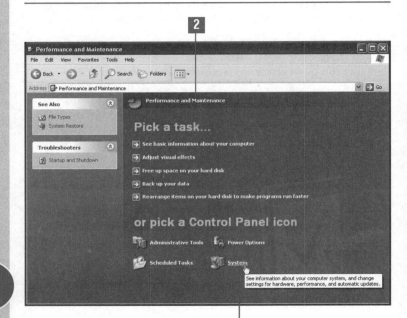

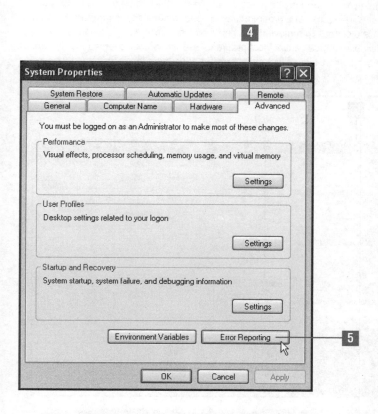

4 Click on Advanced.

5 Select Error Reporting. You will now be able to decide which errors get reported to Microsoft. You can choose to disable the reporting function, or allow reports only on operating system errors, all program errors or those program errors you select.

6 Select the button marked Choose Programs and select the program which was 'not responding'.

7 Click OK to finish.

For your information

To make changes to the system you must be logged on as an administrator. When an error occurs, a dialog box will be displayed, prompting you to indicate whether or not you want to report the problem. When you choose to report the problem, technical information about the problem is collected and then sent to Microsoft over the internet. If other people have reported a similar problem, and more information is available, a link to that information will be provided.

If a system error occurs, displaying a blue screen, the error reporting dialog box will be displayed after you restart your computer.

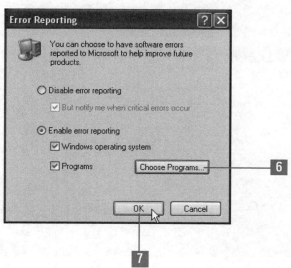

Dealing with crashes 57

Deleting temporary files to regain storage space

One of the consequences of a crash can be that your computer becomes the repository of lots of temporary (temp) files. Most programs use temp files while you are working on a document. These files can be auto save files or just working files. If a program crashes and terminates the program it will not have a chance to remove these files which can, over time, build up and use valuable storage space. Most programs use the Windows temporary directory to store these files. It is a simple matter of deleting these files and regaining the space.

1 Click on Start.

2 Click My Computer icon to open the My Computer window – from here you can access all of your computer drives.

3 Click to the hard disk icon called Local Disk (C:).

4 If you get the message 'These files are hidden', click Show the contents of this folder.

Did you know?

The first time you enter the local disk window you will not be able to see any files or folders. These files are kept hidden from view as you can do some damage if you don't know what you are doing.

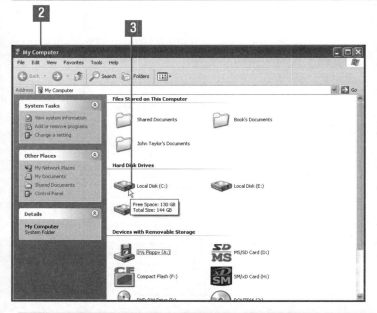

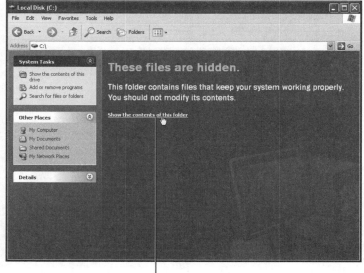

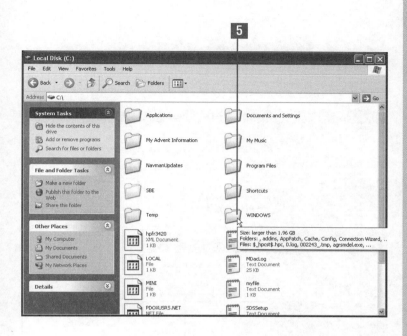

5 Double click on the folder marked Windows.

6 If necessary, select Show the contents of this folder so that you can see what's there.

7 Open, by double clicking on it, the folder called Temp.

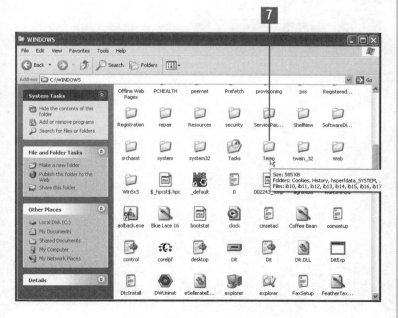

Jargon buster

Directory (often referred to as folder) – a way of organising a collection of files on your computer's hard drive or other media into separate compartments, much in the same way as drawers in a filing cabinet. The main directory is called the root directory, with all the other sub-directories stemming from it. You can organise files in a directory in many ways, such as alphabetically, or by type, size or date.

Folder – what Windows uses to organise all the files. Think of them like the filing cabinets in an office, a way of keeping relevant files grouped together for easy access.

5

Deleting temporary files to regain storage space (cont.)

8 To select multiple consecutive files, select the first file with a left click.

9 Press the Shift key on the keyboard and click on the last file you want deleted. (This will select all files between the two clicks.)

10 Right click on any one of the selected files.

11 Select Delete from the pop-up menu.

12 Confirm that you do want the files deleted by clicking on Yes.

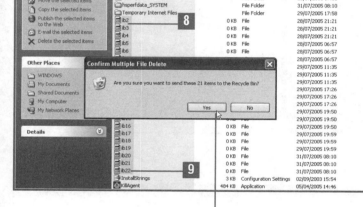

Important

Make it a point to read the dialog box, as it is a good habit to get into. This box is Windows giving you a second chance. Don't get in the habit of just selecting OK. The day will come when you will not want to delete a file as you have made a mistake.

Microsoft has provided the Help and Support Center, which is a comprehensive resource for practical advice, tutorials, and demonstrations to help you learn to use Microsoft Windows XP. Use the search feature, index, or table of contents to view all Windows Help resources, including those that are on the internet.

Using the Help and Support Center you can:

1 Let a friend help you over the internet by using Remote Assistance.

2 Research which hardware and software is compatible with Windows XP.

3 Get help online from a support professional by using Microsoft Online Assisted Support.

4 Undo changes to your computer by using System Restore.

5 Use tools such as System Information to manage and maintain your computer.

6 Stay up-to-date with the latest support information and Help news from sources such as Microsoft Product Support Services and your computer manufacturer.

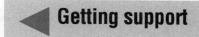

Getting support

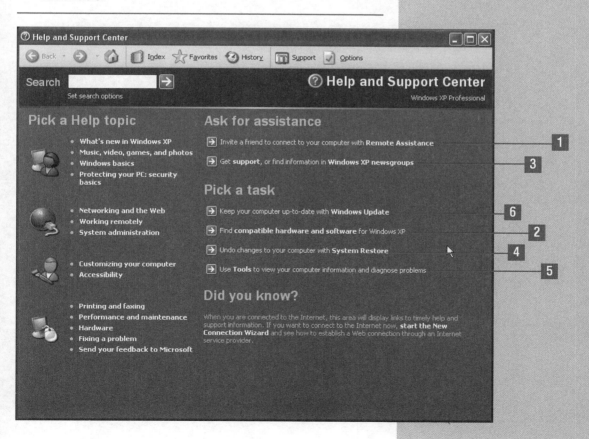

Startup problems

Introduction

In this chapter we will be looking at what happens when the computer first starts up. You will learn about the POST routine, what the BIOS does and how it can alert you to hardware problems. We will also look at the diagnostic tools that are available to us if we startup in Safe Mode, and cover the steps that you can take to help identify software and hardware problems.

What you'll do

Understand what happens when your computer starts up

Understand what happens when you switch on

Start Windows in diagnostic mode

Use diagnostic tools

Correct a video mode

Stop problem programs from running at startup

Trace hardware problems

Understanding what happens when your computer starts up

Assuming that the machine switches on, makes a noise and even displays something on the monitor, it is still possible for it not to continue its start-up or 'boot' sequence. Whenever you switch a machine on it performs a short test to make sure that everything is reasonably OK. This test is called the Power On Self-Test or POST.

The POST test is designed to cater for situations in which a machine is so damaged that it won't even have a working video display. In these instances the POST will often beep at you to tell you what is wrong. The beeps are produced through the small loudspeaker that every PC has and not via the sound card or its attached loudspeakers. These beep error codes are about the only time that this loudspeaker is used.

The beep codes aren't completely standard, depending on which company made your computer's BIOS (Basic Input/Output System) chip, but in most cases if you hear anything other than a single beep then your machine is trying to tell you that there is a problem. To find out what the beeps mean you have to look in the manual that came with your machine. If you can't find the manual, or can't find the part of the manual that tells you about beeps, then at least remember what the beeps sounded like: one long, one short, one long, short, long, etc. and tell your dealer.

Most hardware problems that cause beeps are serious and can't easily be fixed. The exceptions are when memory chips or video cards work loose. The solution is to open the case and push everything back into its socket and see if that cures the problem. If this doesn't stop your machine beeping, or you don't feel up to opening its case, then it needs to go back to the supplier or the manufacturer for repair.

For your information

Even if you don't hear extra beeps, the POST can still halt the machine with an error message displayed on the screen.

Jargon buster

BIOS – Basic Input/Output System can be found on your computer's motherboard. It controls the most basic operations and is responsible for starting your computer up and checking all hardware attached to the computer.

POST (Power On Self-Test) – the check that every computer runs when it first powers up, to ensure that all necessary hardware is present and correct.

AMI BIOS beep codes

The following are AMI BIOS beep codes that can occur.

Beep code	Description
1 Long	DRAM memory failure
2 short	Memory parity failure problem with memory
3 short	Base memory 64K RAM failure
4 short	System timer failure
5 short	Process failure faulty motherboard
6 short	Keyboard controller on motherboard is faulty
7 short	Processor error
8 short	Graphics card memory Read/Write test failure
9 short	ROM BIOS checksum failure
10 short	CMOS error
11 short	Cache memory error

AWARD BIOS beep codes

These are Award BIOS beep codes that can occur.

Beep code	Description
1 long, 2 short	Indicates a graphic card error, the BIOS cannot initialise the video screen to display any additional error messages
Constant beeping	Memory problem

Understanding what happens when your computer starts up (cont.)

For your information

Because of the wide variety of different computer manufacturers with these BIOS chips, the beep codes may vary.

Jargon buster

Memory – areas which the computer's main processor uses to store, manipulate and run programs. The amount of memory a computer has is measured in megabytes or gigabytes. The more you have the more you can do.

RAM (Random Access Memory) – provides temporary storage for files that are in use. RAM is volatile memory and loses the data held when power is switched. Windows and other software require large amounts of RAM to operate.

6

Understanding what happens when you switch on

When your computer is first switched on the first program to run is contained in the BIOS chip. This software configures the computer's hardware and runs the POST test. It then runs a program called the Boot Loader. This allows you to choose which operating system you are going to use when more than one system is installed on your PC, e.g. Windows XP Home edition or Linux. Finally it looks for the operating system on the disk drives connected to the computer, in the order specified in the BIOS. This is usually:

1. The A: floppy drive.

2. The C: hard drive.

3. The D: CD-ROM drive.

If Windows is present, this will then take over the startup process. It can fail for both software and hardware reasons at this stage. As part of the loading process it checks the hardware and then loads the drivers for the hardware. If it loads an incompatible or corrupt driver, Windows can stop in its tracks. Windows then moves on to loading programs that have been configured to load at startup. This can include antivirus programs, internet programs, fire walls and spam programs. Startup programs can take a long time to get up and running and can contribute to slow startup times.

Finding out about POST and what it does

Each time the computer boots up the computer must past the POST. Here is a list of the tests carried out:

1. The power supply is turned on and that releases its reset signal.

2. CPU must be in place, reset and be able to execute instructions.

3. BIOS must be readable.

4. BIOS checksum must be valid. This checks for changes or corruption.

5. CMOS be ready for reading.

6. CMOS checksum must be valid.

7. CPU can read the memory such as the memory controller, memory bus and memory module.

8. The first 64 Kb must be working and be capable of being written to and read.

9. Input/Output bus/controller must be accessible.

10. Input/Output bus must be able to read the video card and video RAM.

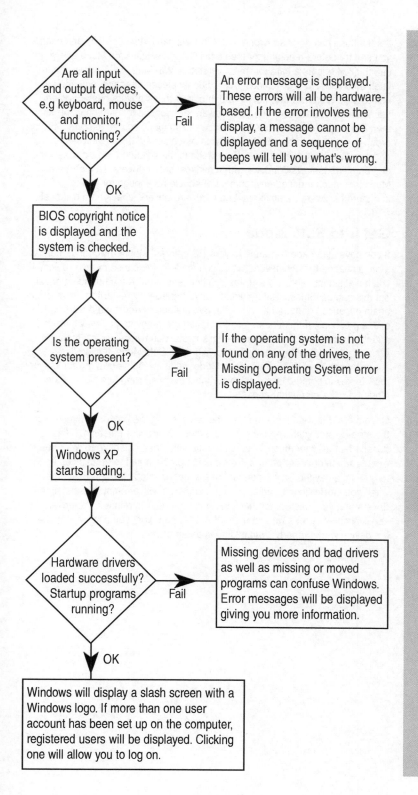

Are all input and output devices, e.g keyboard, mouse and monitor, functioning?

Fail → An error message is displayed. These errors will all be hardware-based. If the error involves the display, a message cannot be displayed and a sequence of beeps will tell you what's wrong.

OK

BIOS copyright notice is displayed and the system is checked.

Is the operating system present?

Fail → If the operating system is not found on any of the drives, the Missing Operating System error is displayed.

OK

Windows XP starts loading.

Hardware drivers loaded successfully? Startup programs running?

Fail → Missing devices and bad drivers as well as missing or moved programs can confuse Windows. Error messages will be displayed giving you more information.

OK

Windows will display a slash screen with a Windows logo. If more than one user account has been set up on the computer, registered users will be displayed. Clicking one will allow you to log on.

For your information

Windows can restart unexpectedly or freeze. If this happens suspect a virus.

6

Starting Windows in diagnostic mode

If something has gone so wrong that Windows can't start, there is an option you can try before reaching for the install CD. It's called Safe Mode and you can think of this as a bare minimum version of Windows. As Windows loads itself onto your PC it also loads the additional pieces of software needed to talk to the PC's hardware, i.e. drivers. If one of these drivers has a problem because it isn't intended for your hardware or because it is set up incorrectly then it is possible for this to stop Windows loading. Of course to correct the problem you have to be able to start your machine and this is impossible because Windows doesn't load! Safe Mode is the solution to this chicken and egg problem. It starts Windows with a minimal set of drivers. Though Safe Mode is a much reduced environment, it should be enough for you to configure hardware, remove any bad hardware drivers, check hard disks, etc.

Get into Safe Mode

If you have just made a change to your PC before it stopped working, there is a good chance that whatever change you made is the cause of the problem. If you have just installed a driver, the solution is to remove the offending driver, but this can be difficult. Before you do anything else try restarting the machine again because Windows has an automatic method of removing drivers which cause problems. If this doesn't work you can try removing any new hardware and then restarting. If your machine fails to start up twice in a row then Windows should automatically try starting up in Safe Mode. If even this doesn't work, start Windows in Safe Mode manually, hold down the F8 key, or the Ctrl key in some cases, while your machine is starting and select Safe Mode from the menu that appears.

See also

See 'Identifying hardware problems using Device Manager' on page 7.

See also

See Chapter 7, 'Fixing BIOS problems'.

Once started in Safe Mode remove the driver using the Device Manager – see the step-by-step guide on page 7 – and then restart your machine. If this doesn't restore your machine to full functionality then you have to work out exactly which driver or other software is the problem and to do this you need to go a little beyond Safe Mode and use a step-by-step startup. Notice that when you start Windows again in normal mode, it will attempt to reinstall the drivers that you deleted. You have to refuse the offer to reinstall the drivers to see if Windows works without them. If it does now work you can try to make the device work properly by installing updated drivers.

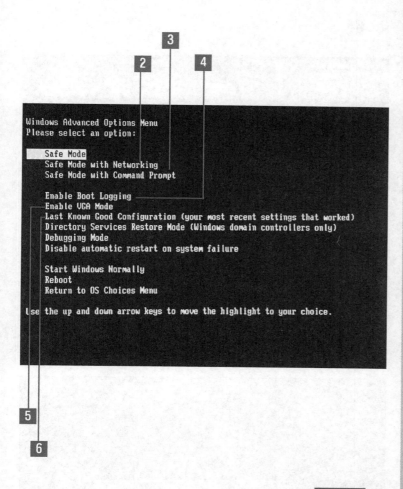

```
Windows Advanced Options Menu
Please select an option:

    Safe Mode
    Safe Mode with Networking
    Safe Mode with Command Prompt

    Enable Boot Logging
    Enable VGA Mode
    Last Known Good Configuration (your most recent settings that worked)
    Directory Services Restore Mode (Windows domain controllers only)
    Debugging Mode
    Disable automatic restart on system failure

    Start Windows Normally
    Reboot
    Return to OS Choices Menu

Use the up and down arrow keys to move the highlight to your choice.
```

Choose Start mode

1 The first option on the list is Safe Mode. For this task you need to select this option. Hold down the Ctrl key or press F8 to see the Windows startup menu.

2 Safe Mode with Networking – if you need to access a network while in Safe Mode, use this option. To do this, use the down arrow key on your keyboard to highlight this selection and press the Enter key.

3 Safe Mode with Command Prompt – this option will start Windows in Safe Mode and then load a DOS window which will allow you to use the DOS shell to issue commands to your computer.

4 Enable Boot Logging – will produce a list of the actions taken when loading Windows. This list can be useful to track down exactly where Windows stops working.

5 Enable VGA Mode – sets the graphics display to the lowest common denominator and should be used if you are having problems with the graphics display.

6 Last Known Good Configuration – is a useful option, Windows will load earlier settings and this can fix many problems.

! Important

Timing is important. Push the key just after the POST test. It is possible to miss this timing and Windows will attempt to load normally. If it does, just turn off the computer and try again.

6

Starting Windows in diagnostic mode (cont.)

Load Safe Mode drivers

1. As Windows starts up in Safe Mode it prints to the screen each of the files it is processing. This can be a large list which scrolls past very quickly.

2. Once Windows has finished the first loading section it will display a warning dialog box tell you about Safe Mode.

3. To continue to load in Safe Mode click on the Yes button.

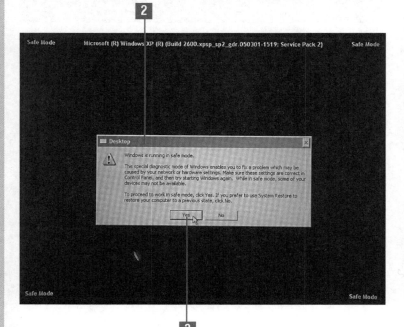

1

2

Safe Mode Microsoft (R) Windows XP (R) (Build 2600.xpsp_sp2_gdr.050301-1519: Service Pack 2) Safe Mode

Recycle Bin

My Bluetooth Places

Safe Mode Safe Mode

Start 06:33

2

Safe Mode desktop

1 Windows will now start in Safe Mode.

2 You can always tell that Windows is in Safe Mode because of the change in the video display and the Safe Mode messages in each corner of the screen.

Jargon buster

Safe Mode – a minimal operating version of Windows, which should always work unless there are serious hardware problems.

6

Using diagnostic tools

The biggest problem with Safe Mode is that it might very well get your PC started but it doesn't give you much help in finding out what is actually causing the problem. If you can start your PC in Safe Mode the only thing you can be sure of is that the majority of your PC's hardware is working properly. You can run almost the same range of diagnostic programs as in normal mode to help you find the fault. Some of the most important ones can be found on the Tools menu of the System Information utility.

System Information

1 In Safe Mode you can also make use of all of the standard diagnostic tools.

2 Open the Start menu, select All Programs, then Accessories, then System Tools.

3 Click on System Information to start the program.

4 System Information is packed with facts about your computer. You can use it to find hardware conflicts, check memory usage and check on individual devices.

5 Click on the plus icon to open up that branch and find out more information about hardware resources, components, software environment, internet settings and applications.

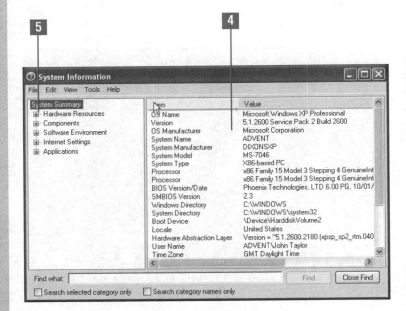

One of the most common problems that requires Safe Mode to solve, is the selection of an incorrect video mode. If you select a video mode that is supported by your PC's video hardware but not by the monitor, then your PC will work but you will not be able to see anything on the screen due to the rolling and tearing of the picture. You can fix this problem if you start in Safe Mode.

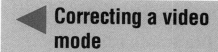

Correcting a video mode

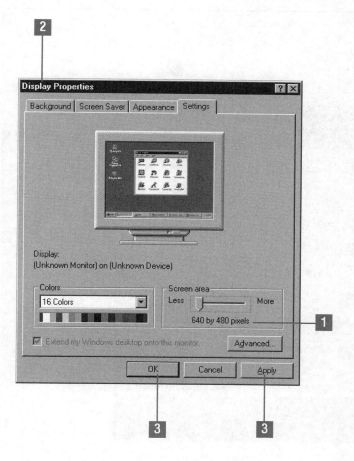

1 Restart in Safe Mode which always uses a 640 x 480 16-color graphics mode which works with any monitor.

2 Open the Display Properties dialog box – right-click anywhere on the desktop and select Properties.

3 You can't change video mode in Safe Mode, but you can change the mode for the next start up. Click Apply or OK, which changes the video mode to 640 x 480 in 16 colors the next time you start up in normal mode.

4 After the next start up, use the Display Properties dialog box to set the graphics mode you actually want to use.

6

Stopping problem programs from running at startup

You can use System Configuration to undo some harmful changes to your computer and stop programs automatically running at startup. The System Configuration utility helps automate the troubleshooting steps that Microsoft product support services technicians use when diagnosing Windows configuration issues. You can use this tool to modify the system configuration and through a process of elimination with check boxes, find troublesome programs. System Configuration must be started in a different way to most Windows programs.

Run MsConfig

1 Click the Start button then click Run at the bottom of the second column.

2 The Run menu allows you to run programs by typing in the name.

3 Click into the box marked Open and type in the name of the program you want to run, in this case MsConfig.

4 Click OK.

For your information

Left clicking on the down arrow to the right of the Open box will drop down a list of previously run programs. This is a useful shortcut that saves you retyping the program name.

Important

You must be logged on as an administrator or a member of the administrators group in order to use System Configuration. If there is only one user account on your computer, that will also be the administrator's account.

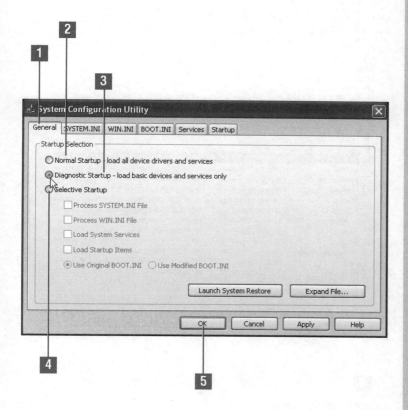

Stopping problem programs from running at startup (cont.)

Select Startup modes

1 The General tab allows you to select different startup modes.

2 Normal mode is the default setting and in this mode Windows starts up as standard.

3 Diagnostic mode loads basic services and devices only. This allows you to bypass troublesome drivers and programs, which would otherwise stop Windows loading.

4 For this task choose Selective startup, which allows you to choose which programs and services load on startup. You can use this to stop programs you no longer need starting or to eliminate troublesome programs by a process of elimination.

5 Click OK.

?

Did you know?

You can also select which services load on startup by clicking on the Services tab and repeating the steps shown.

6

Stopping problem programs from running at startup (cont.)

Startup programs

1 The Startup tab has a list of the programs which will run when Windows starts up. Click on its label to bring this tab to the front.

2 Every program with a tick in the left-hand side box will be loaded at startup.

3 To stop a program loading, click in the box to remove the tick.

4 When you have finished, click OK.

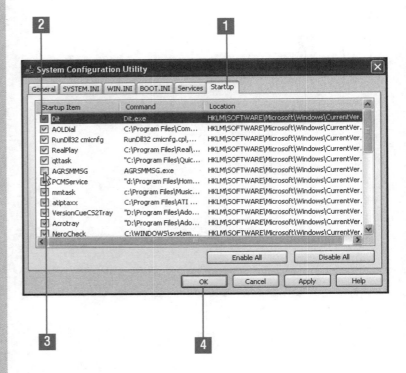

Timesaver tip

If you want to turn off all but a few essential startup programs, it is quicker to click Disable all and turn on the ones you want.

Add Hardware would not necessarily be the first place you would think of if you were diagnosing hardware problems, but you can use it to find hardware already connected to your computer and then use a troubleshooter tailored to that hardware to diagnose it.

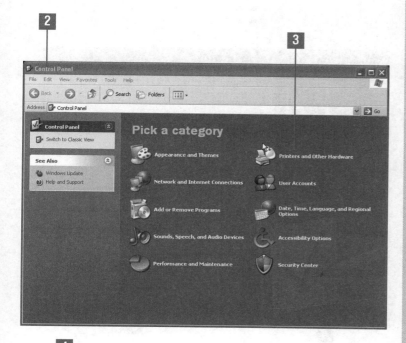

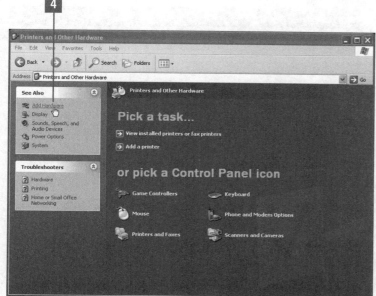

Tracing hardware problems

Start hardware troubleshooters

1 You can start a hardware troubleshooter by first working through the Add Hardware Wizard.

2 Open the Start menu and select the Control Panel icon.

3 Click on the Printers and Other Hardware icon.

4 At the Printers and Other Hardware menu, click Add Hardware.

Timesaver tip

You can also reach the hardware troubleshooters through the Help and Support Center. At the opening page take the Hardware link, then select Fixing hardware problems.

Tracing hardware problems (cont.)

Work through

1 Now you need to work through the Add Hardware Wizard.

2 Click Next.

It's connected already

3 As we are troubleshooting a piece of hardware we will assume it is already connected.

4 To tell the Wizard, click the Yes radio button to select it.

5 Click Next.

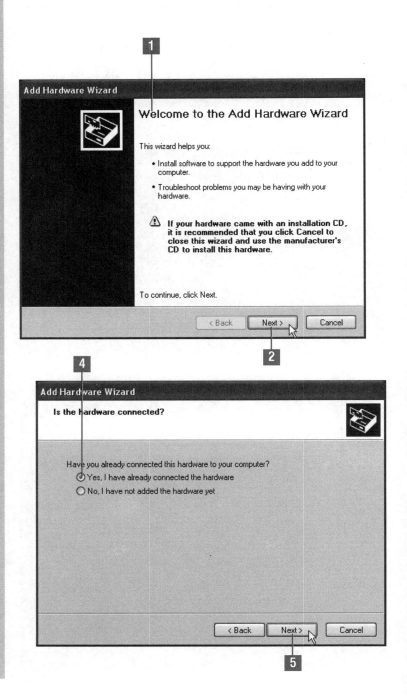

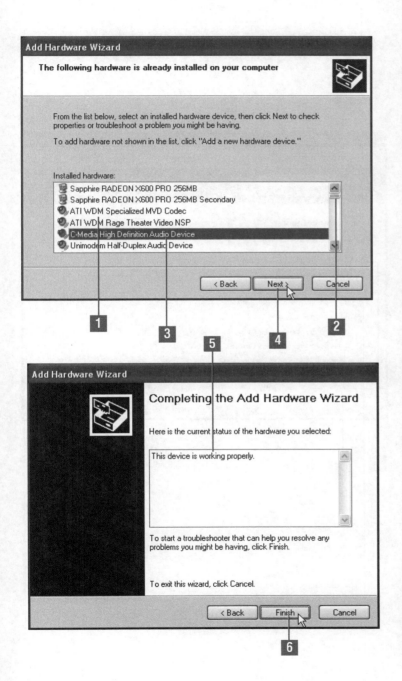

Select the device

1 A list of the hardware already installed on your computer will be displayed.

2 The scroll bar to the right of the box can be used to move though the list.

3 When you have found the hardware you want to troubleshoot click on the name to select.

4 Click Next.

Finish the Wizard

5 The Add Hardware Wizard will now display the status of the hardware you selected.

6 To finish, click Finish. You might be forgiven for thinking you have not done anything, but what you have done is select the hardware that the troubleshooter will be based on.

6

Tracing hardware problems (cont.)

1 The Help and Support Center is now launched, pre-selected for trouble-shooting the device you selected in the earlier steps.

2 The troubleshooter will present you with a selection of multiple-choice questions.

3 To select an answer, click the radio button next to the question that is closest to a description of your problem.

4 Click Next.

5 The wizard will take you through several similar screens as it attempts to identify and solve the problem.

For your information

You will be presented with a series of questions until troubleshooter arrives at a solution or runs out of options.

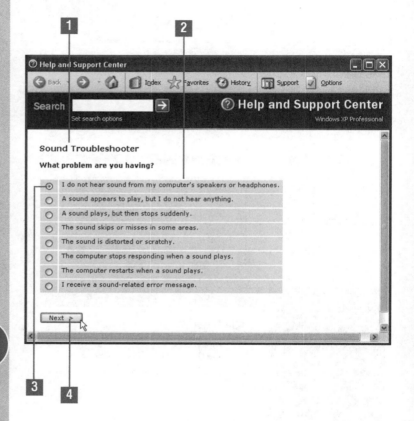

Fixing BIOS problems

7

Introduction

The BIOS is a small program that controls the Basic Input/Output System on your computer. The program is stored on a small chip called an EPROM (Erasable Programmable Read-Only Memory). This chip can be found on the computer's motherboard. When a computer is first switched on you may be surprised to learn that Windows is not the first program to run. Every time a computer is switched on it needs to know what makes up the computer. It needs to know it has hard drives, floppy disks, memory, add-on devices, etc. This information is stored in the EPROM chip along with basic configuration for all devices connected to the computer. The EPROM and its program collectively store their information in a chip called CMOS (Complementary Metal Oxide Semiconductor) memory. This chip stores information used by the BIOS and holds this information even when the power is turned off, unlike the main system memory, which forgets everything as soon as the PC is switched off. CMOS memory is an old technology that needs a battery to keep the information in the chip. Effectively the chip never gets switched off. A small battery on the motherboard powers the chip even when the computer's power is turned off. This is where things can go wrong. Batteries can fail or simply run down and when they do the CMOS chip loses all its stored information and the computer can't start, as it has no idea what kit it has. This means it doesn't know it has a hard drive, so it can't look for the drive and start loading Windows.

All computers come with the BIOS installed. The PC manufacturer's place relevant information and pre-configure the BIOS to suit each individual PC. These settings are usually the failsafe settings. You can use the BIOS to tweak your PC and to get better performance. There are several BIOS manufacturers and each BIOS is different and many can be updated with a Firmware update allowing you to make sure your PC can make use of new technologies. In conclusion the BIOS is a computer program. It tells your computer about all the devices connected to it. As part of the startup process the BIOS checks the devices to see if they are working – this is the POST test discussed in Chapter 6. The program's function is to look for devices, making sure they are still attached to the computer, and pass this information to Windows via the processor.

What you'll do

Look at the BIOS

Use Advanced BIOS settings

Set a password

Reset factory defaults

Looking at the BIOS

You have probably seen the black and white images that flash up when your computer starts up. Each of these messages has a meaning but they flash by so fast you normally don't get a chance to read them. There are several stages in this phase of startup, which allow you to branch off the normal startup sequence. To do this you not only have to press the right key but you have to do it at the right time. Every BIOS manufacturer in the early days used a different key or set of keys. These days there is now a degree of standardisation. This means the first keys to try are the Del key or the F2 key.

1 Your computer will actually tell you which key to use but the message is displayed so fast you might need to start your computer several times to catch it.

2 The first screen you will see is the main menu for the CMOS Setup utility. This screen will look very different if you have only been used to Windows.

3 The menu is divided into two columns. The first column contains menu choices for configuration of CMOS, BIOS and device settings.

4 The second column allows you to set passwords, load default factory settings and save changes.

5 This section explains how to use the menu.

6 The bottom section of the menu gives a brief description of each menu selection.

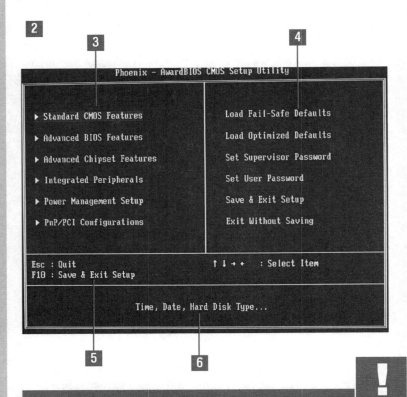

Important

Be very careful when changing anything in the BIOS and never change anything unless you know what effect it is going to have. Making changes in the BIOS is not like making changes in a program where you can try it and see what happens. It's very easy to totally mess up your computer! Always read your computer manual first. If you do make a change that stops your computer working, the only way to restore your BIOS and CMOS is to pull the battery from the motherboard and the chip will forget everything including your changes. This of course means you will have to start from scratch.

Date, drives and CPU

```
                 Phoenix - AwardBIOS CMOS Setup Utility
                         Standard CMOS Features

    Date (mm:dd:yy)          Tue, Aug  9 2005            Item Help
    Time (hh:mm:ss)           5 : 57 : 41
                                                   Menu Level   ▶
  ▶ Primary IDE Master     [PIONEER DVD RW  DVR-]
  ▶ Primary IDE Slave      [IDE DVD-ROM 16X]        Change the day, month,
  ▶ SATA 1 Master          [WDC WD1600JD-00HBB0]    year and century
  ▶ SATA 3 Slave           [ None]
  ▶ SATA 2 Master          [WDC WD1600JD-00HBB0]
  ▶ SATA 4 Slave           [ None]

    Drive A                 [1.44M, 3.5 in.]

    Video                   [EGA/VGA]
    Halt On                 [No Errors]
    BIOS Version             2.0E (01/10/05)
    CPU                      Intel(R) Pentium(R) 4
    FSB/Multiplicator        3.40GHz (200x17.0)
    Cache                    1024K
    Total Memory             1024MB (DDR 400Mhz)

 ↑↓→←:Move  Enter:Select  +/-/PU/PD:Value  F10:Save   ESC:Exit  F1:General Help
    F5: Previous Values    F6: Fail-Safe Defaults   F7: Optimized Defaults
```

1 The first option on the CMOS setup menu is the Standard CMOS Features section. To select this option use the keyboard arrow keys and navigate the menu using the up and down keys. As this is the first section on the menu you should leave the red highlight on the Standard CMOS Features option and press the Enter key on the keyboard to select it.

2 The date and time can be changed here, but it's much easier to do this in Windows.

3 The next section is a list of drives connected to your computer. On older systems if this information was lost you would have to manually re-input this information. The CMOS can now automatically search for this drive information. It is, however, a good idea to take notes.

4 The Video section is now largely redundant. It allows you to select EGA or VGA graphics adaptors. No computer sold in the last 10 years has been fitted with an EGA graphics adaptor.

5 Again this option is now more or less redundant – you don't want your computer halting every time there is an error.

6 The final section is an inventory of the processor, memory and cache as well the BIOS version.

Using Advanced BIOS settings

1 The Advanced BIOS Features menu allows you to tailor your computer's system and optimise it either for Windows XP or a different operating system.

2 Quick Boot bypasses some of the POST test for a faster startup.

3 Security Option allows you to set passwords and protect the boot sector of your hard drive. This field allows you to limit access to the System and Setup. The default value is Setup. When you select System, the system prompts for the user password every time you boot up.

4 Boot Sequence allows you to choose which storage device is looked at first for the operating system. Many computers look at the floppy drive first, this is a throw back to the days when PCs used to boot from floppies. Changing this setting so the hard drive is looked at first will save valuable seconds. There are circumstances when you may want to boot from a CD-ROM first.

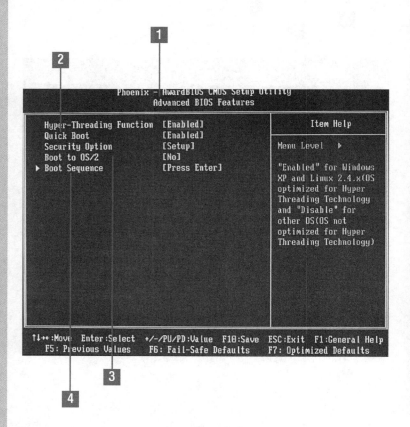

```
              Phoenix - AwardBIOS CMOS Setup Utility
                    Advanced Chipset Features

   Memory Hole             [Disabled]              Item Help
 ▶ PCI Express Root Port Func[Press Enter]
                                               Menu Level   ▶




 ↑↓→← :Move  Enter:Select  +/-/PU/PD:Value  F10:Save  ESC:Exit  F1:General Help
    F5: Previous Values     F6: Fail-Safe Defaults    F7: Optimized Defaults
```

```
              Phoenix - AwardBIOS CMOS Setup Utility
                      Integrated Peripherals

   USB Controller           [Enabled]              Item Help
   Onboard USB Mode         [USB 2.0]
   USB Keyboard Support     [Enabled]           Menu Level   ▶
   USB Mouse Support        [Enabled]
   Azalia/AC97 Selection    [Auto]
   Onboard VIA 1394         [Enabled]
   Onboard LAN              [Enabled]
   Onboard Lan Boot ROM     [Disabled]
 ▶ IO Devices Configuration   [Press Enter]
 ▶ IDE Devices Configuration [Press Enter]
 ▶ SATA Devices Configuration[Press Enter]




 ↑↓→← :Move  Enter:Select  +/-/PU/PD:Value  F10:Save  ESC:Exit  F1:General Help
    F5: Previous Values     F6: Fail-Safe Defaults    F7: Optimized Defaults
```

Use Chipset Features

1 The Advanced Chipset Features list will depend on the chipset on your motherboard. Some lists are longer than others.

2 The Memory Hole setting is now redundant. Some pre-plug-and-play expansion cards required access to particular memory addresses in order to function properly. This option lets you set aside the appropriate area of memory for these cards. This setting should be disabled unless you have a card that you know requires this setting.

3 PCI Express Root Port Function allows you to enable or disable this function.

View built-in devices

4 The Integrated Peripherals list will again depend on the motherboard fitted in your PC.

Many motherboards come with built-in graphics, modems, LAN cards and sound cards, for example.

5 These devices can be enabled or disabled. If, for example, you upgraded your computer with a high-end sound card, you would then want to disable the built-in sound device, as you only need one. This will also stop the two sound devices clashing and fighting for resources.

Fixing BIOS problems 85

Using Advanced BIOS settings (cont.)

Get the power

1 This field is related to how the computer is switched on – such as with the use of a conventional power button.

2 Wakeup Event Setup; on many computers you can choose to have the computer wakeup on the activation of the LAN, a modem, USB or even a keyboard event.

It's all for display

3 By default, the BIOS initialises the PCI Slot VGA when the system boots. Once again the BIOS shows its age as there are very few, if any, PCI-based graphics cards on sale today. Most cards are now AGP and you might want to set your system to initialise this slot first.

4 This option allows you to enable or disable ESCD.

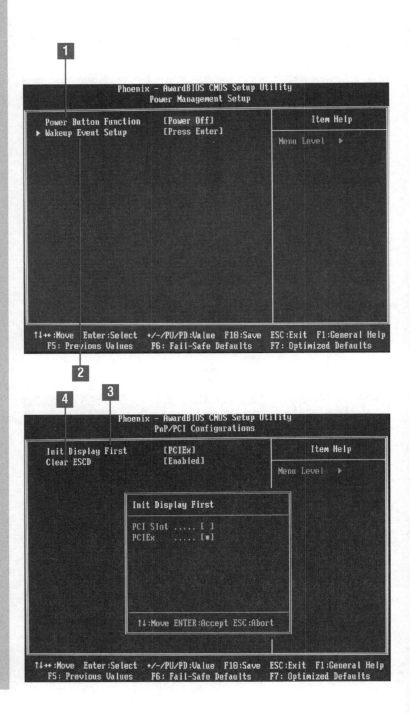

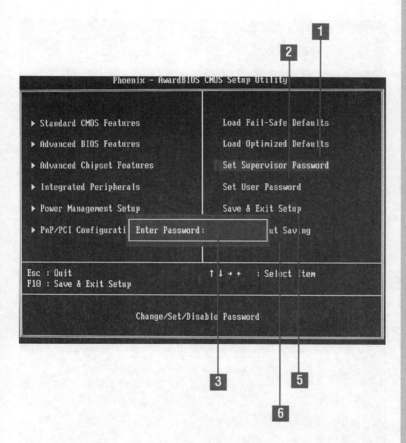

Phoenix - AwardBIOS CMOS Setup Utility

▶ Standard CMOS Features
▶ Advanced BIOS Features
▶ Advanced Chipset Features
▶ Integrated Peripherals
▶ Power Management Setup
▶ PnP/PCI Configurati

Load Fail-Safe Defaults
Load Optimized Defaults
Set Supervisor Password
Set User Password
Save & Exit Setup

Enter Password: ut Saving

Esc : Quit
F10 : Save & Exit Setup

↑ ↓ → ←   : Select Item

Change/Set/Disable Password

1 The set supervisor password option sets the system password. This password will be used to protect your computer and Setup utility.

2 User password sets one that will be used exclusively on the system. To set a password, select the option from the menu and press Enter.

3 The Enter Password box is now displayed and a message asks you to enter the password. Type your password, entering up to eight characters. When you are done press the Enter key. After setting a password, the screen will return to the main menu.

4 To disable a password, leave the box blank and press the Enter key when you are prompted to enter the password.

5 Save & Exit Setup. This option allows you to determine whether or not to accept the modifications. If you type 'Y', you will quit the Setup utility and save all changes into the CMOS memory. If you type 'N', you will return to the Setup utility.

6 Exit without Saving. Select this option to exit the Setup utility without saving the changes you have made in this session. Typing 'Y' will quit the Setup utility without saving the modifications. Typing 'N' will return you to Setup utility.

Resetting factory defaults

This option is really a troubleshooting mode. The CMOS is loaded with factory set default values. These settings are permanently stored in the BIOS ROM. These default settings will disable all high-performance and advanced features and return your computer to a state where it should function if you have gone a tweak to far.

Use safe settings

1 The Load Fail-Safe Defaults option is one of the simpler menus; it's a two option choice – yes or no. Choosing yes will load a basic factory set of options for the entire CMOS, so this simple action has powerful consequences.

2 Press the 'Y' key on your keyboard to select and OK the action.

Use optimal settings

3 This option is also a troubleshooting mode. This time a tried and tested set of optimised settings will be loaded into the CMOS from the BIOS ROM. Choose this option if you want a safe but optimal set of settings.

4 Press the 'Y' key on your keyboard to select and OK the action.

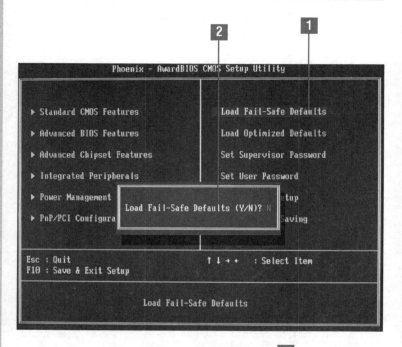

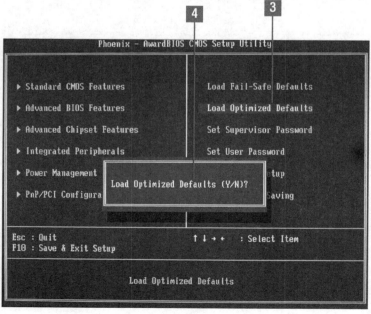

Memory

Introduction

If memory fails, it is likely to do so quickly. Sometimes memory can be dead on arrival – doomed even before you get the computer home or it can fail when you add an upgrade or make some other change.

In this chapter we will look at why memory may fail, what to do if it does, and how to find and fix common memory errors.

What you'll do

Learn about memory errors

Use basic checks for memory faults

Install the memory

Add memory

Track down a faulty memory module

Explore memory types

Important

If your new computer is having memory errors, leave the problem to your computer supplier to fix, especially if the computer is still under guarantee. If you try to fix the problem you may invalidate your guarantee.

Learning about memory errors

If you've installed new memory and experience problems, you may have installed the wrong memory. Double-check the part numbers. Confirm that you have configured and installed the memory correctly.

If you have just recently installed or removed hardware and you're now getting memory error messages, try looking inside the computer case. You may have dislodged a connection during the installation or knocked the memory chip out of its socket.

If you've just installed some new software or upgraded your operating system, and are getting new memory errors bear in mind that new software, though new, is not bug free and beta versions are notorious for producing memory errors. Always check the software manufacture's website for upgrades and patches for your software. As a final resort, contact the memory manufactures technical support team, they may already know of the problem and have a fix.

If your system has been running fine, but over time becomes unstable with more and more memory errors reported, it is most likely to be a hardware problem, since software configuration and installation problems show up as soon as the computer turns on. This sort of hardware problem is usually made by overheating and can be caused by a problem with the computer's power supply, or by dirt and corrosion in the connection between the module and the socket. If this is the case remove the memory and clean the socket with a soft cloth or cotton bud.

See also

Beep codes, page 65 and Tracing hardware problems, page 77.

Jargon buster

Memory – areas which the computer's main processor uses to store, manipulate and run programs. The amount of memory a computer has is measured in megabytes or gigabytes. The more you have the more you can do.

RAM (Random Access Memory) – provides temporary storage for files that are in use. RAM is volatile memory and loses the data held when power is switched. Windows and other software require large amounts of RAM to operate.

For your information		
RAM mMemory requirements for all Windows versions		
OS Software	minimum requirements	recommended
Windows XP Professional	128 MB	512 MB
Windows XP Home	128 MB	512 MB
Windows 2000	128 MB	512 MB
Windows ME/98	64 MB	256 MB

Here are some of the things that can go wrong with memory and why.

If you have just upgraded make sure you have the right memory part for your computer. You can look up the part number on the manufacturer's website. Many memory manufacturers have configurators which allow you to select your computer from their database. Alternatively, phone the memory manufacturer, consult your computer manual, or phone the computer manufacturer. Finally, if you are not sure, take one of your existing memory chips to your local computer shop and ask them to supply you with new memory compatible with your existing memory.

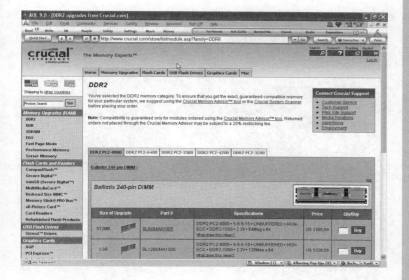

Timesaver tip

The computer may inform you of a memory problem at startup, in three ways.

The computer won't boot, merely beeps (POST test). The computer boots but the screen is blank. The computer displays a memory error.

For example:

1. Memory mismatch error.

2. Memory parity error.

3. Memory verify error.

4. Memory address error.

5. Memory failure.

Installing the memory

Many computers require module installation in banks of equal-capacity modules. Some computers require the highest capacity module to be in the lowest labelled bank. Other computers require that all sockets be filled; some need memory to be installed in pairs. You can look up your computer requirements in its manual or check your computer manufacturer's website for technical support.

1 Installing memory can be tricky. Because some memory models install by leaning the card back then clicking it upright you will have to install the front chip first.

2 Make sure the module is firmly pushed into the socket. You will feel it click home when the chip is in position.

For your information

For older computers try updating the BIOS. Older BIOSs may have an upper limit on how much memory they can access. Many computer manufacturers update BIOS information frequently – you can find new versions on their websites, usually under the support section.

In this task you will learn what memory looks like and where to find it on the motherboard. It is simple to replace faulty memory or to add more memory. Adding memory is a cost-effective way of upgrading and speeding up your computer.

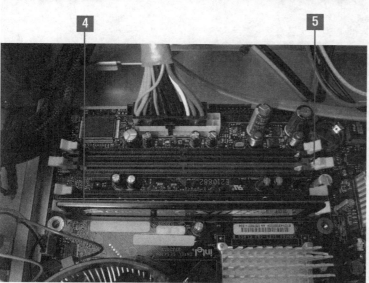

Use color coordination

1 Memory banks can be found on the main motherboard.

2 These memory banks are color-coded. The blue banks need to be filled first.

3 Make sure you have clear access to the memory banks by temporarily and carefully taping cabling out of the way.

Prepare the ground

4 Your computer will have at least one memory module already installed.

5 Locate the memory bank you are going to put your new memory in and pull back the retaining clips on either side. Be careful, the clips have been known to break off, but if you are careful you should be fine.

Insert your new memory

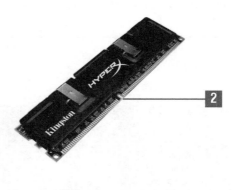

1 Now insert your new memory module in its slot.

2 There is a notch in the center of the card and a bump in the socket. These are set slightly off center so the module will only go in one way. This means you can't get the module in the wrong way around.

Make sure it's in

3 Push the card firmly down in the socket and as you do the retainer clip will start to close.

4 While pushing in the card, also push the retaining clips home. Do not force the clips. If they are not closing, check you have the module the correct way around and the card is fully in.

The best way of tracking down faulty memory is to use a process of elimination. What you are trying to do is prove which memory modules definitely work and which you're not certain of. This requires a methodical approach to work through all possibilities. The more modules you have, the more difficult the task. Finding out which one of two modules is faulty is, on the other hand, very simple.

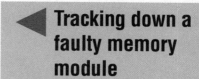

Tracking down a faulty memory module

1 Remove the new memory and see whether the problem disappears.

2 Remove the old memory, reinstall the new and see whether the problem persists.

3 Try the memory in different sockets. Swapping reveals whether the problem is a particular memory module or socket, or whether two types of memory aren't compatible.

Did you know?

When adding more memory to your computer this tip will save you money in the long run. Buy the biggest memory chips you can afford. It is far better to have two 512 memory chips and leave two slots free in your system, than buy four 128 memory chips and fill your computer's slots. You save money because once you have filled your computer's slots you have to remove some of the existing memory to make room for new, higher-capacity chips. If you have free slots you can upgrade again, just pop new memory in and you don't have the problem of what to do with your old memory that you paid good money for.

Exploring memory types

SDRAM

DIMMs (Dual In-line Memory Modules) have a 64-bit pin connection. DIMMs modules are fast 168-pin, 10 ns SDRAM. 100 MHz SDRAM DIMMs will work with motherboards supporting Intel Pentium II and Pentium III 350 MHz and above CPUs.

133 MHz DIMMs are suitable for Intel Pentium III and AMD K7 Athlon systems.

DDR

DDR (Double Data Rate) SDRAM DIMMs. They offer twice the bandwidth of normal SDRAM meaning that they perform twice as fast. DDR DIMMs offer an overall improvement to system performance. DDR SDRAM DIMMs are compatible with newer Intel Pentium 4 and AMD Athlon-based motherboards.

RDRAM

RDRAM RIMMs are specially designed to work with Pentium 4 systems. Operating at 800 MHz it is far faster than normal SDRAM. RIMM is not backwards compatible with older systems.

EDO

EDO (Extended Data Out) RAM are 72-pin SIMMs with channels suitable for older Pentium systems. EDO RAM is not suitable for 486 (or earlier) machines. SIMMs are 32-bit, 72-pin, non-parity with a 60 ns access time. All Pentium PCs require SIMMs in pairs.

Hard drives

Introduction

The primary storage solution for any PC is the trusty hard disk. Hard disks come in various sizes from the now entry-level 40 GB to 100 GB with the top-of-the-range 500 GB models. The difference here is massive and it's sometimes difficult to know how much space you really need.

The very large hard drives would really only be useful to someone who is doing either video or music editing or using their computer as a personal video recorder. A 40 GB drive would be a good size for the average user to start with; it will allow you to install a large amount of applications and games and still have room to archive your MP3s and digital camera snaps. However, the price difference between a 40 GB and a 100 GB drive is now very small – for just a few pounds extra you can buy yourself the extra room. There is one possible use for having an oversized hard disk, and that is to partition it. Creating an extra partition will produce a second virtual drive, which Windows will consider to be a separate piece of hardware. The advantage with a partitioned drive is that you can back up your hard disk using a program like Norton Ghost – although there are other programs available. What Ghost does is to create an image file of everything on your hard disk, so that if something catastrophic happens, a restore from the image will take just a few minutes rather than hours. Just remember that a partition is not a separate piece of hardware and that if the drive itself breaks all the data will be lost. This section covers simple hard drive maintenance — what to do if your hard drive fails.

What you'll do

Learn how a hard drive works

Use Disk Cleanup

Speed up a tired drive

Use data recovery companies

Recognise data recovery dos and don'ts

Learning how a hard drive works

A hard drive stores data magnetically – this means that it changes the magnetic polarity of particles on the disk to either positive or negative values. This is considered by the read head as a stream of binary bits, i.e. either 0 or 1. The inside of a hard disk consists of a series of magnetic disks, usually two or three, which are connected to a central spindle and spun round at high speed by an electric motor.

A series of read/write heads extend into the drive like the arm on a record player. These heads can either add data by changing the polarity of the particles on the disk or simply read what is already there. The data on the disk is structured in a series of concentric circles called tracks. These are split up into wedge-shaped sections called sectors; the final index is the side of disk being written to. You may have seen errors where a side X sector X track X error is mentioned in the text. This is because the view you normally have of the disk is carefully constructed to be easy to use and not necessarily represent the storage on the disk.

Hard drive data layout

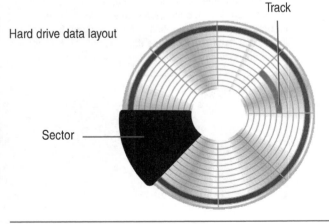

Track

Sector

Jargon buster

Sector – division of a disk. Sectors are grouped into tracks. The boot sector of a disk is the first sector, and is used to start the operating system.

It doesn't matter how large your hard drive is, you will fill it eventually. When you do your computer will slow down and you will find it difficult to run your programs. In this task you will find out what to do when the hard drive is full. Windows XP has a wizard called Cleanup that will help you remove the clutter safely from your hard drive. When you run out of space this cleanup wizard will be started automatically by Windows to help you out. However, here we will be starting the wizard manually.

Using Disk Cleanup

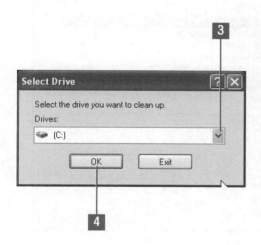

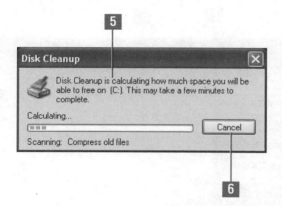

1 To start the Disk Cleanup wizard, open the Start menu, and select All Programs, then Accessories, then System Tasks.

2 Click Disk Cleanup to start it running.

3 If you have more than one disk connected to your computer, you will be asked to select the disk you want to clean. Click the down arrow to the right of the box and select the drive from the drop-down list.

4 Click OK once you have selected the drive you want to work on.

5 Disk Cleanup will now scan your drive and work out how much space it can free up. This may take a while depending on the size of your drive. Wait until it has finished.

6 You could at this point decide not to continue with the cleanup operation. Click Cancel if you want to end the wizard.

9

Using Disk Cleanup (cont.)

How much space?

1 When finished Disk Cleanup will display a dialog box showing what files can be safely removed.

2 The wizard will place ticks in some of the boxes for you.

3 You will need to select any other files you want to be removed. To do this, click on the box next to the set of files you want removed. A tick will be placed in the box.

4 A description of what the files are and what they do is displayed to help you decide what stays and what goes.

5 To view the files that Disk Cleanup has selected. Click on View Files.

Where are these files?

6 The View Files option starts off by showing the folders the files are stored in. You can, however, browse these files and folders, as you would normally do.

7 This is the location of the files.

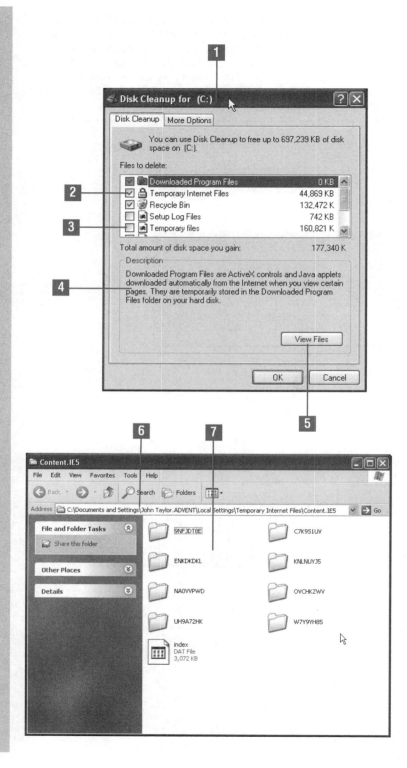

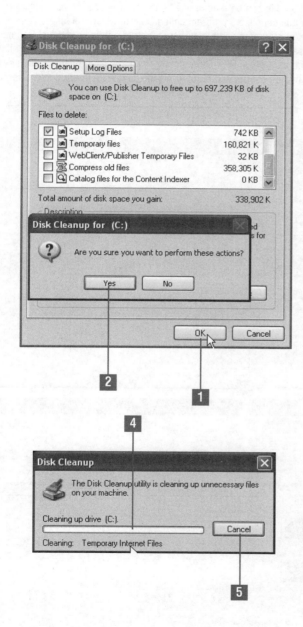

Clean those files

1 Once you have selected the files you want to remove, all that remains is for you to click OK.

2 The wizard will give you one more chance to back out of the action – as you want to continue, click Yes.

3 The Disk Cleanup wizard will now remove the files from your hard drive and free up some valuable space.

4 A progress bar lets you know how much of the task is completed.

5 You could still cancel the task at any point by clicking the Cancel button.

9

Speeding up a tired drive

In this task you will defragment the files on your hard drive. With use, the files on any hard drive can get spread all over the place, the file itself can be broken down into segments and placed in different locations on the drive. This has the effect of slowing down hard drive access time and this happens because the read heads on the hard drive have to search for the files. The time they take to physically move to the location of the file slows down the access. If the file can be read in one hit the file will be read much quicker. Microsoft has supplied a program called Defrag, which will take these segments of programs and place them together on the hard drive. Segmented files are said to be fragmented and the job of Defrag is to defragment all the files on the hard drive. Disk Defragmenter can check and defragment any hard drive connected to your computer – this includes both internal and external drives.

Defragment files

1 Start Disk Defragmenter from the All Programs > Accessories > System Tools menu.

2 Click on the drive you want to defragment.

3 Click Analyze to check the drive. This will show you how fragmented the drive is and what it is likely to look like after defragmentation. If your drive does not require defragmenting Windows will let you know at this point.

4 To start the defragmentation process click Defragment.

5 Once defragmentation has finished you should have a disk that looks like this one. The blue section shows contiguous files. Any fragmented files would show up red and immoveable files would be green.

Jargon buster

Defrag – (defragment). Fragmentation is where files are split into multiple parts around a hard disk. When you defrag, the file system joins these fragmented parts back together, or at least moves them closer to each other, so that the hard disk has less work to do when searching.

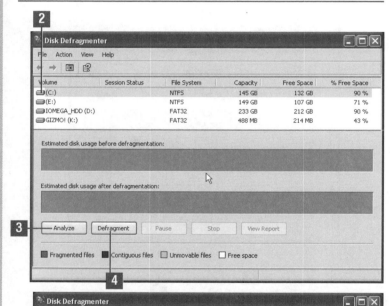

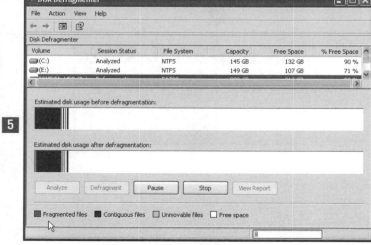

We all assume hard drives are indestructible and we trust our most precious data to them. *Don't!* They are not indestructible. You must assume your computer's hard drive is going to fail one day and you must be prepared for the day when it happens!

There are many problems that may require you to seek a data recovery service; the following examples are just some of the more common problems:

Computer won't boot, formatted hard drive, applications that are unable to run or load data, malicious data loss, file saved but cannot be located, power surges, hard drive/media surface contamination and damage, hard disk/drive component failure, accidental deletion of data, virus attack, corrupt files/data, operating system upgrades, clicking/whirring noises, hard drive seen in the BIOS but not recognised in Windows, accidental reformatting of partitions or hard drive, fire or water damage to hard drive or media.

In most situations where data is lost there is a possibility of recovery. If the drive has simply stopped functioning or even if the drive has completely crashed the data can be recovered. Data recovery experts have experience of recovering data from most types of media, many from physically damaged disks.

Data recovery is often required after environmental damage from fires, floods, or other physical damage to a disk or drive. There are many companies who can offer data recovery services. The following is a sample.

Ontrack Data Recovery

http://www.ontrack.co.uk

If you find yourself with one of the aforementioned problems, try a data recovery company, as this is one problem you're not going to be able to fix yourself.

Ontrack Data Recovery is a well-established company who provide a reliable service. Their staff can talk you through the recovery process and will provide you with all the information you need to have your data recovered.

Ontrack's engineers can recover inaccessible data from virtually every operating system, storage device and data loss situation.

Disklabs

http://www.disklabs.com/index.asp

Data recovery specialists and computer forensics experts based in the UK, Netherlands and New Zealand. If you have lost your data, it may not be as bad as you think.

Disklabs have a wealth of experience in computer forensics and critical data recovery and are able to recover almost any type of data loss, from almost any media type. They can even recover data after fire and flood damage.

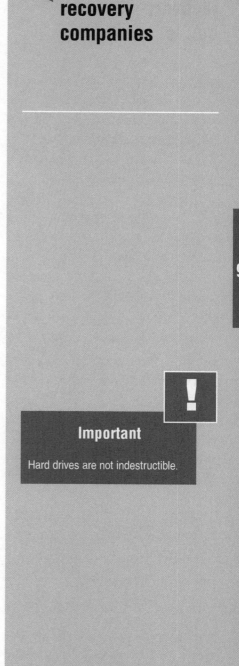

Using data recovery companies

9

Important

Hard drives are not indestructible.

Recognising data recovery dos and don'ts

Never assume that your data is completely lost!

Do backup your data.

Do make sure you check your backup works.

Do turn the computer off immediately if you hear clicking or whirring noises coming from the hard drive – then contact a data recovery company.

Do stay calm and get help, there is a very good chance your data will be recovered. More files could be lost through panic measures than anything else.

Don't start up the hard disk/drive again as this will cause more damage.

Don't use your computer in extreme hot or cold environments.

Don't use your computer in a high humidity/wet environment.

Don't be tempted to shake or hit a drive that has problems, any loose heads or debris will damage the record surface and make things worse.

Don't open your hard disk/drive yourself.

Don't attempt to format your drive or change the partitions when you are unable to access your files.

CD-ROMs

Introduction

It is not uncommon to have problems with a CD-ROM or DVD. The trouble with these disks is that they are fragile and unprotected, and can easily get scratched and dirty. All but the most minor scratches, dirt, and especially greasy fingerprints can make it difficult for the laser in the CD drive to load and read files on the disk. However, careful handling and good care of disks should help prevent disk-related problems. On the other hand, some cases just need simple remedies. Plain soap and warm water will take care of the most common problem – greasy fingerprints. If, however, you have the misfortune to get a scratch that stops the disk being read, you may need specialist disk rescue services. The use of such a service can help polish out the scratch if it's not too deep. You can even buy scratch removable gadgets at your local supermarket – however, these will only deal with minor scratches.

Dirt can also make its way into the disk drive itself. Don't be tempted to go poking around with a cotton wool bud, as the lens of the drive is very delicate. You can clean the drive using CD cleaner kits which consist of a cleaning disk and some cleaning fluid. Always invest in a CD cleaning kit to clean the disk drive itself.

Disks now come in a dizzying array of formats, including CD-ROM, CD-R, CD-RW, DVD, DVD+R, DVD-R, DVD+RW, DVD-RW, Blue ray and dual layer. However, they all have several things in common.

1. They all have a read surface that can be scratched.

2. They all have a pigment surface used to record the information.

3. They all have a top surface.

What you'll do

Check the drive configuration

Check volume settings

Important

To prevent disks from being scratched, always hold the disk with your fingers around the circumference – and do not touch the surface.

Always put your disk in its storage case as soon as you have finished with it.

Never write on the top surface with a hard pen, only ever use specially designed pens. Any scratching of the top surface, no matter how small, will cause irrevocable damage. This is because the recording pigment is on the other side of the top surface.

Checking the drive configuration

You can check the drive configuration with Device Manager and its related tools and utilities.

1 Open the Start menu and right-click on My Computer. Select Properties at the bottom of the menu.

2 When the System Properties dialog box appears, select the Hardware tab. This section contains the Device Manager, Windows Update and hardware menus.

3 Choose Device Manager.

Select DVD/CD-ROM drives

4 The Device Manager dialog box is now displayed. This box contains a list of all the devices connected to your computer.

5 Each icon has a plus in a little box next to it, which indicates there is more information to be displayed.

6 Click on the plus box next to the DVD/CD-ROM drives icon.

7 Each drive connected to your computer is now displayed.

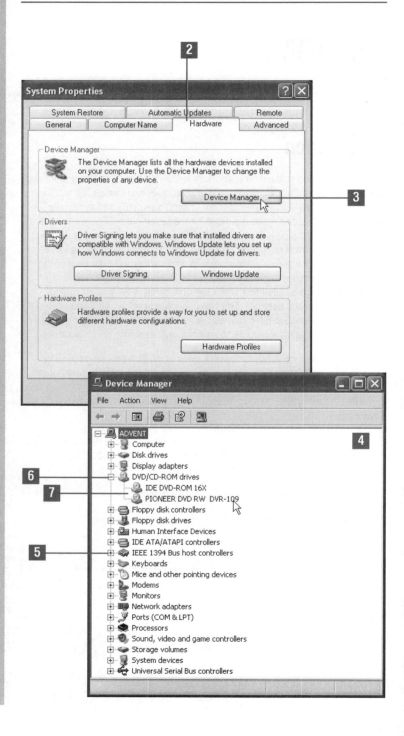

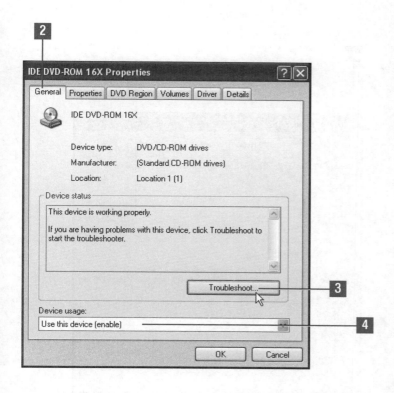

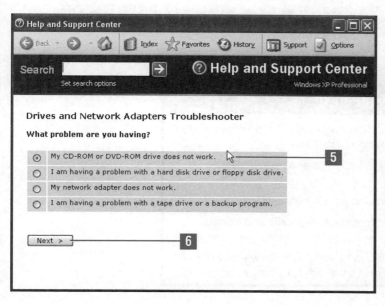

Use the device properties and troubleshooter

1 Double-click on the drive you want to select to bring up the Drive properties box.

2 Each of the tabs displays different information about the drive. Select the General tab.

3 Click on the Troubleshooter button to start the troubleshooter for your selected drive.

4 You can also use the General tab to disable this device if you suspect a clash with another device.

Use the drive's troubleshooter

5 When the Help and Support Center troubleshooter is displayed, you need to select the CD-ROM or DVD-ROM option. Click in the radio button to select it.

6 Click Next and work through the troubleshooter.

Checking the drive configuration (cont.)

Use the volume control

1 If you are having trouble with sound coming from the drive, you can adjust the player volume in the Properties tab of the drive's Properties dialog box.

2 Click the Properties tab.

3 To adjust the volume click and drag the slider to the desired volume.

4 You can also enable digital CD audio in this screen.

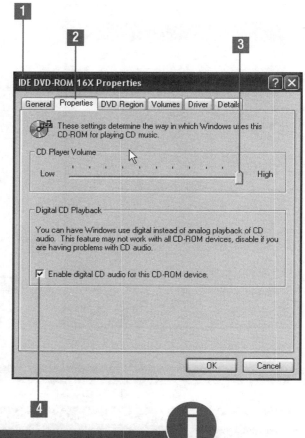

For your information

Cleaning a disk is safe isn't it? Well no – you could do more damage if it is not done correctly. It is, however, worth doing if you are having trouble mounting a drive.

1. Make sure you don't use water that is too hot as this can cause damage to the disk. Lukewarm water is fine.

2. Don't apply the soap directly to the disk as this can scratch the disk surface.

3. Gently clean the surface of the disk with your fingertips. Move your finger in a circular motion and cover the entire surface.

4. It is important to rinse the soap off the disk thoroughly. Run the disk under the cold tap to make sure all traces of soap are removed. Finally, dry off with a soft cloth or kitchen towel.

Windows XP also has a master set of volume controls. These are set out in the form of a mixing desk. The desk has the volume controls for all sound devices attached to the computer, including the CD-ROM drive. This same volume control can be set to mute devices. If this option is set then no sound can come from the CD-ROM drive.

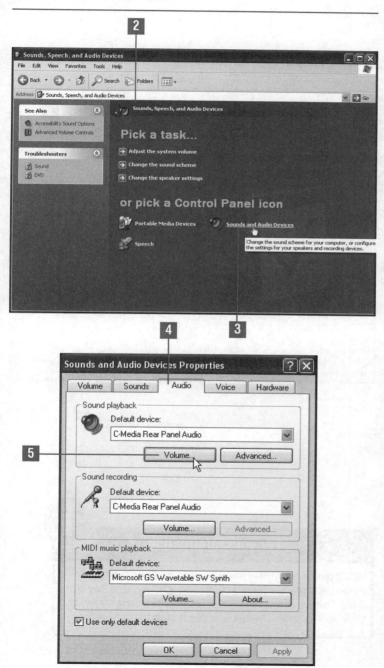

1 Click the Start button and select Control Panel.

2 Click the Sounds, Speech and Audio devices link.

3 Click on the Sound and Audio Devices icon.

4 Select the Audio tab.

5 Select the button marked Volume.

10

Checking volume settings (cont.)

Volume control

1 The volume of the CD-ROM drive can be changed by using the slider control. Click and drag on the slider knob till you hear the required volume.

2 At the bottom of each slider is a check box. If the check box has a tick in it, it means the device is muted and no sound will come out. If it is a toggle switch, you can mute and unmute by clicking in this box. To make sure there is sound you need to clear this box.

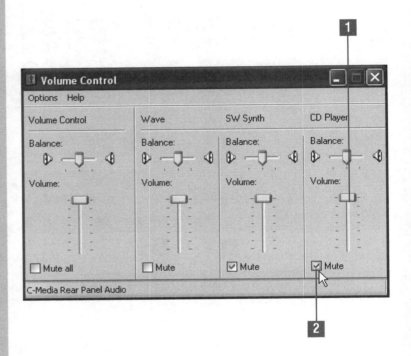

For your information

Muting can be set by other programs using Windows. They can do this automatically and some don't ask you or tell you what they are doing. So if you have recently installed any software and the sound stops working on any device it is worth checking the mute setting.

Video display

Introduction

Today's graphics cards are mini computers in their own right, they have a processor and their own memory. Most have a cooling fan and their own configuration software. Many graphics cards even come with over-clocking software to make the card work faster.

Graphics cards can go wrong in a number of ways, from a simple change in resolution, making your icons huge and your desktop cramped, to a blank screen. Most graphics problems can be fixed via Windows using software. However, if you get the dreaded blank screen you can't see to fix the problem. If you do get a blank screen then first go through the obvious checks. Is your computer plugged in and switched on? Is your monitor plugged into the graphics card? Is the monitor switched on and does the monitor work? When you have exhausted all the obvious checks, you're left with a graphics card problem. If the card has malfunctioned the POST test will pick this up and beep a sequence of beeps to tell you it's the graphics card that's faulty. A blank screen can mean one of two things; a hardware fault, in which case you will need to try a new card, or a software fault. If you have recently updated the graphics card drivers, the driver may have become corrupted. Again, you are going to replace your graphics card but only temporarily. Windows will auto-detect the new card and load drivers for it. Once you can see Windows again you can uninstall the driver for the malfunctioning card.

What you'll do

Control graphics using software

Find out what screen savers do

Learn what to do if the monitor is blank

Change the look of Windows XP

Controlling graphics using software

This task will take you through some of the fixes you can do using software. You can use the graphics properties menu to make changes to the way Windows looks, but you can also change video modes and video settings.

Access desktop properties

1 Right-click on any blank section of the desktop and select Properties from the pop-up menu.

2 The Display Properties dialog box is now displayed.

3 The Themes tab lets you change the way Windows looks using preset Themes and is a simple way to make your Windows look different.

4 The Desktop tab allows you to change the way the desktop looks.

5 The tab marked Screen Saver allows you to choose one of the many screen savers which will be displayed if you leave your computer switched on when not in use.

6 For this task you need to select the Settings tab.

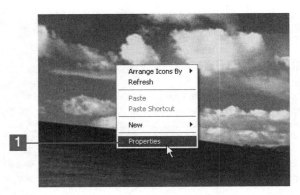

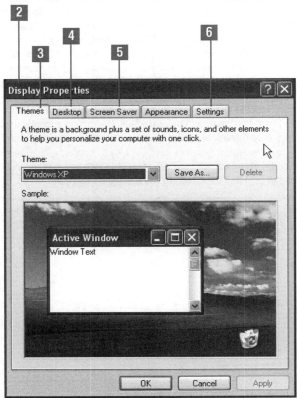

Did you know?

Screen savers were originally more than pretty moving pictures. Screen savers were just what the name suggests. They saved your monitor's screen from an affliction called burn-in. If the same image was displayed on a monitor screen for a very long time, the image was permanently burnt into the screen. You can see this on some older bank cash machines. Burn-in does not tend to happen on home computers so screen savers are just a bit of fun.

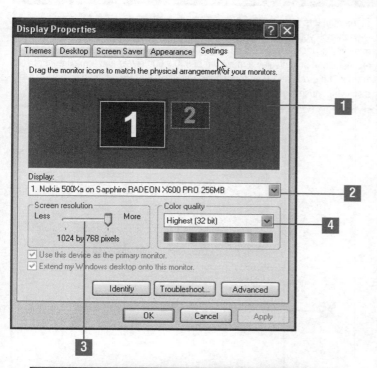

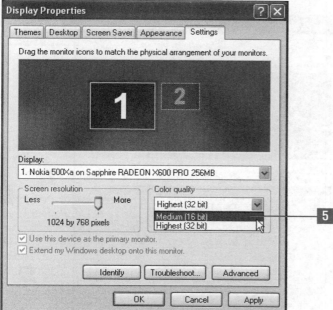

Double display

1 If you have two graphics cards and two monitors Windows can deal with each of them and allow you to configure the way they display Windows.

2 The Display box allows you to select which monitor you are working with. This is not present if you have only one monitor connected.

3 The Screen resolution box shows you the current screen resolution.

4 The Color quality box shows how many colors the graphics card is set to display.

Color quality

5 To change the color quality, click the down arrow to the right of the Color quality box and select from the list.

11

Did you know?

The highest color depth (32 bit), puts the most strain on your card and will slow it down. However, most games require you to run in this mode. The lowest color depth is the basic VGA setting using only 256 colors.

Controlling graphics using software (cont.)

Screen resolution

1 Changing the screen resolution is as simple as turning up the volume on your music centre. Click on the slider knob and drag it to your required resolution.

Monitor drivers

2 It is possible to have one monitor connected to your computer and a choice of drivers to control it. If you are having trouble with your display, try using a different driver.

3 Click the down arrow to the right of the Display box.

4 The drop-down list will display the available drivers. Click on the driver you want to use.

5 If you want to investigate the advance setting click the Advanced button.

Did you know?

640 x 480 pixels is the minimum resolution and this size combined with 256 colors and 8 bits is called VGA mode. As this mode does not use any of the advanced features of your graphics card it is a good mode to troubleshoot in.

For your information

Some monitors are only capable of displaying a limited range of resolutions, even though your card is capable of displaying higher or lower resolutions, the monitor's driver will limit how much you can change it. The Nokia 500Xa, for example, can only display a minimum of 800 x 600 pixels and a maximum of 1024 x 768 pixels and even though the Radeon X600 PRO is capable of displaying much higher resolution, you will not be allowed to select them.

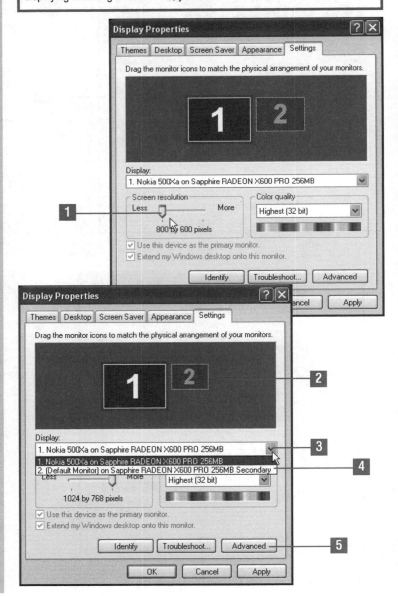

114

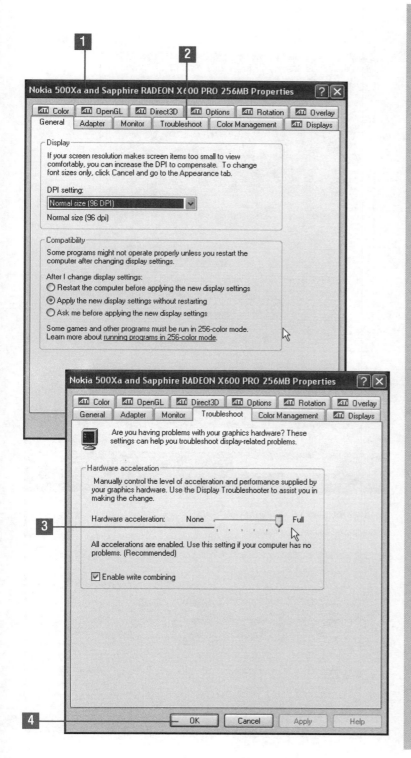

Controlling graphics using software (cont.)

Use Advanced Settings

1 The Advanced Settings dialog box changes depending on what graphics card you have and the monitor you are using with your computer. You do need to know what you are doing to change most settings in this section. It is advisable to read the manuals for both the graphics card and monitor before changing any setting.

Graphics acceleration

2 There is one tab that should look familiar and that is the Troubleshoot tab. Click on it to bring it to the front.

3 The Troubleshooting dialog box is actually quite simple. All it does is turn on and off the graphics cards onboard acceleration. If you are having problems with the graphics display such as random crashes that freeze the display, try turning the acceleration off. To do this, move the slider all the way to the end of the scale with none written to the left.

4 To finish with the dialog box, click OK.

11

Controlling graphics using software (cont.)

Return to Windows XP

1 To finish using Display Properties and return to Windows XP click on OK.

Help and support

2 There is a Video Display Troubleshooter, which can guide you, step-by-step through the more common problems. This troubleshooter is part of the Help and Support Center found on the Start menu.

3 Select the Hardware link, then the Fixing a Hardware problem item and at the troubleshooter select 'I'm having a problem with a display adaptor'. This will take you to the Video Display Troubleshooter.

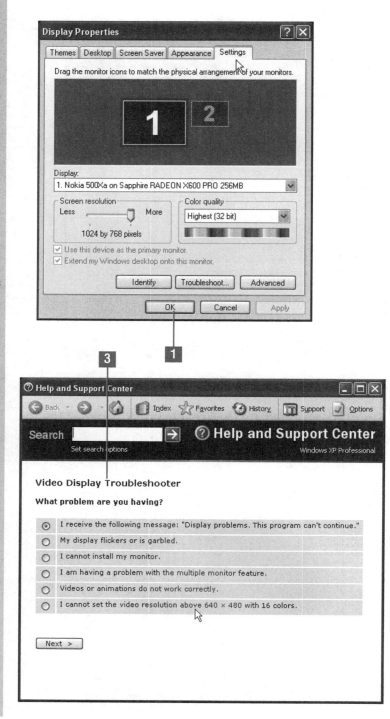

This task is a simple reminder to eliminate the obvious before panicking. If your monitor is blank the most common reasons are either power or connection faults. Other causes of a blank monitor are, for example, the monitor's brightness or contrast could be turned down, though this is highly unlikely as someone would have to physically turn them down. On most modern monitors these controls can be accessed via on-screen menus generated by the monitor itself and each monitor manufacturer uses a different set of menus. For that reason you should read the manual that came with the monitor for instructions on how to operate these menus.

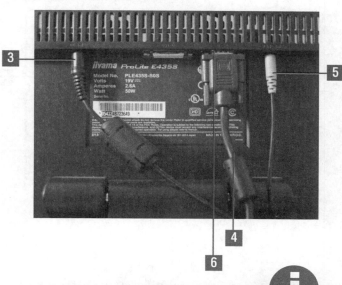

For your information

As the monitor cable is so thick it is quite easy to wrench and dislodge it even if you just slightly move your computer. The plug, which is provided with two screws, fits into the socket. You should use these screws to stop the plug pulling on the socket and bending the pins.

Learning what to do if the monitor is blank

Power to the monitor

1 Lack of power is the most obvious thing to check. Make sure the monitor is plugged in and switched on at the wall.

2 Make sure the monitor is switched on at the power switch on the monitor itself. There is usually an indicator light next to the power switch. If this light is green the power is on and the monitor is receiving a signal from the graphics card. If the light is amber the power is on but the monitor is not receiving a signal from the graphics card so check the connections.

3 Many monitors have three connections. In this case the power connection is the one on the left.

4 The signal connection is the blue plug in the middle, most monitor cables are now color-coded blue.

5 This monitor has built-in speakers and so the sound connection is on the right and is color-coded green.

Check the connection

6 Make sure the monitor cable is firmly pushed into the socket as they have been known to work their way out.

11

Changing the look of Windows XP

Changing the way Windows XP looks may not be rectifying a fault but it can improve not only the way Windows looks but also how it operates. To access Screen Properties click the right mouse button on the desktop in any space not occupied by an icon, menu, dialog box or button. When the pop-up menu appears move the mouse pointer to Properties and click the left mouse button to select.

Change the style

1 Right-click on any blank section of the desktop and select Properties from the pop-up menu to open the Display Properties dialog box

2. Click on the Appearance tab.

3 This window shows an example of the current style and it will change to preview other selected styles.

4 To change to a different style, click the down arrow to the right of the Windows and buttons box.

5 A drop-down list will appear with available styles. Click on a style to select it.

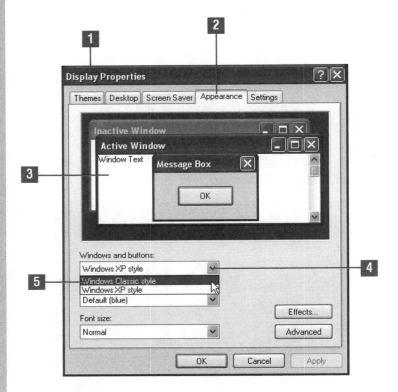

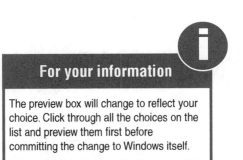

For your information

The preview box will change to reflect your choice. Click through all the choices on the list and preview them first before committing the change to Windows itself.

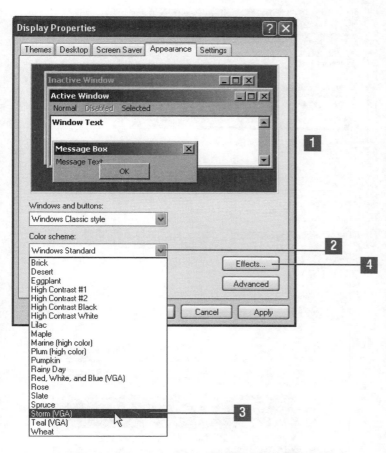

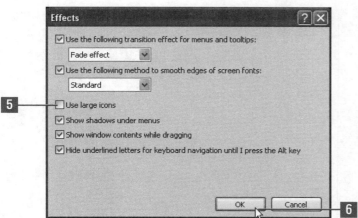

Changing the look of Windows XP (cont.)

Color scheme

1 You can change the color Windows uses for frames, menus and buttons. Microsoft have provided some predefined color sets, including some which will help the visually impaired.

2 Click on the down arrow to the right of the Color scheme box to display its drop-down menu.

3 Click on your chosen color scheme

It's all for effect

4 Windows uses effects to enhance the look of its menus and the effects can be a drain on graphics resources and slow the graphics reaction times. You can turn all the effects off to speed up the graphics display. Click Effects to open the dialog box.

5 To deselect an effect click within a ticked box. The tick will now be removed and the effect deselected.

6 To exit the menu click OK.

11

Changing the look of Windows XP (cont.)

Customize your colors

1 The Advanced button allows you to change the colors of individual elements of Windows.

2 To select the item you want to change click the down arrow to the right of the Item box. A drop-down list is displayed.

3 Click the item you want to change.

Color selection

4 Click the down arrow in the Color box.

5 Now a color palette is displayed. Select your chosen color from this pallet.

6 If you find the color choice limited you can make up your own. Click Other. The Color dialog box will open. Here you can select from a wider palette or mix your own color.

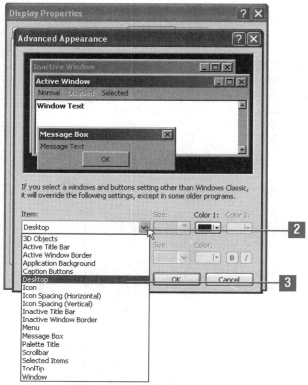

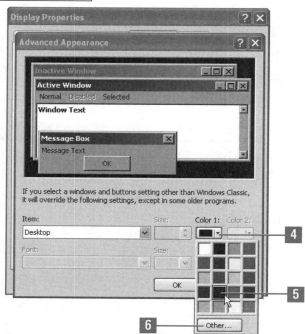

Changing the look of Windows XP (cont.)

Easy to see

1 This is an example of a classic Windows style with an alternate color choice and large icons.

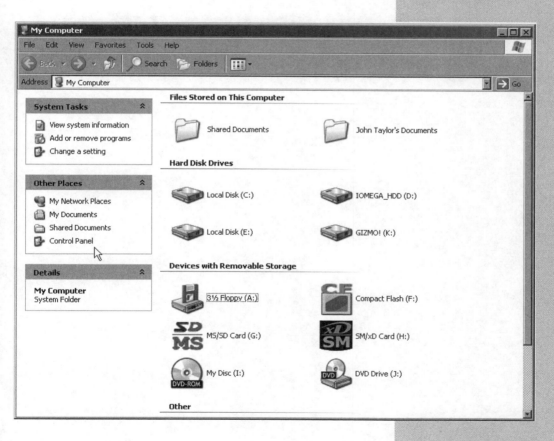

Fixing deliberate damage

Introduction

There was a time when it was virtually impossible for someone to attack your personal computer. Then along came the virus, a malicious piece of software designed to disrupt or disable your computer. Early viruses were spread by passing information around on floppy disks and virus prevention was easy. All that was needed was an up-to-date virus protection program, and your PC would be safe. Unfortunately, this is no longer true. Viruses have evolved, and worms are the result of this development and worms are constantly developing and changing. They target system weaknesses in a tireless quest to gain access to your computer. They travel, not by floppy disk, but through online connections, emails and email attachments. The result is that no one can afford to leave their guard down for a second.

The old antivirus companies have evolved into fully-fledged computer security companies offering much more than just virus protection programs. Virus companies can give you up-to-date information on the latest threats with alerts and newsletters. Many of these companies also provide cleaning programs to remove worms and viruses. While virus protection programs are still very important and useful for protecting your PC, virus protection these days is not about buying virus scanners – it's about buying a complete, multi-faceted service. The following will guide you through the basics and teach you some tactics that will help you keep your PC, and most importantly your data and programs, safe.

What you'll do

Understand protection basics

Be safe online

Identify a virus

Diagnose a virus

Use online virus scanners

Learn about well-known viruses

Remove spyware

Understanding protection basics

With the advent of broadband internet access, many computers are switched on and connected to the internet 24 hours a day, 7 days a week. A computer connected to the internet can be attacked within seconds of connection. This is why you must have a firewall to protect your computer.

With a little thought and preparation you can make your computer safe and secure. Remember that most of the nasty stuff is thrown up by a minority of people, trying to prove a point by finding new ways to cause computer mayhem. More recently virus writers have being trying to make as much money as possible and organised crime is even getting in on the act. Today viruses can be used to steal your identity, your money and your information, blackmail you or con you! You can, however, fight back and here's how.

Check Windows Firewall

1 Microsoft has provided a firewall as part of Windows XP second edition. It is important you use this as minimum protection. It is also worth looking at buying a firewall from a respected data security company.

Jargon buster

Virus – a program that has been deliberately created to cause problems on your computer. Though usually minor they can erase your entire hard disk. Viruses are commonly spread via email as an attachment or by removable storage media (floppies, CDs, etc.). Never open an attachment you are unsure of!

Firewall – a barrier between the internet and your computer. It protects from outside threats like viruses and hackers by filtering the incoming data, blocking any potentially harmful information. Firewalls are an absolutely vital part of any system connected to the internet.

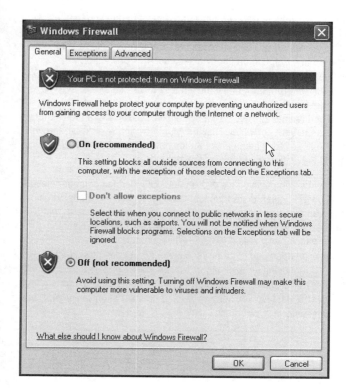

Before you start browsing online, set up two email accounts. Most ISPs will let you have more than one, or you can create a Hotmail or Yahoo account as a secondary account. Only use one account for talking to people you know and the other for any correspondence with people you don't. Just about everything online, from registering programs to joining discussion boards, demands your email address. When you sign up for a service, use your secondary email address to filter all circulars and junk to one place.

Get another email package; Microsoft Outlook and Outlook Express are under constant attack. Microsoft does a good job patching the holes but another answer is to try a package with a lower installed user base. These packages are less popular as targets because they are less widespread. Email packages can have holes punched in them and the virus can trigger without you doing a thing. So eliminate one way of risking your machine by using another email program. Suggested programs include Eudora, Google G-mail, Opera or Firefox, but there are others.

If you plan to download programs from the net, make sure you install a spyware monitor such as Ad-Aware to make sure that nothing naughty is lurking in the background behind your new utilities. Spyware can now get on to your computer in many ways. Simply visiting a site can trigger a download of spyware. Some computers connected to the internet have been known to be riddled with spyware.

Don't be afraid of buying on the internet but do be careful. If you intend to make financial or personal information transactions over the internet, always look for the padlock symbol being closed at the bottom of the browser. This means a secure connection has been made.

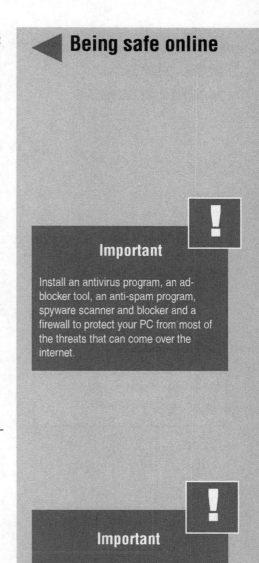

Being safe online

Important

Install an antivirus program, an ad-blocker tool, an anti-spam program, spyware scanner and blocker and a firewall to protect your PC from most of the threats that can come over the internet.

Important

Never ever give out personal, financial or sensitive information on internet chat sites or forums. No one will ever ask you for registration codes or passwords except people running scams, or hackers after your details.

12

The answers to some common security problems

Q. Is Windows more vulnerable than Linux?

A. No. In terms of actual security lapses in each of the systems they are as secure and insecure as each other. However, Microsoft gets targeted more as there are many more installations of Windows than Linux. Therefore, there are greater opportunities to cause more mayhem by writing a Windows virus.

Q. What is a virus hoax and what should I do?

A. Virus hoaxes are usually caused by a trickster trying to spread panic about a non-existent virus (this can be as damaging as a real virus). Very often you will hear about a virus from a well-intentioned friend via email.

Q. When online, how often are you subject to a hacking attempt?

A. Tests have been carried out on firewalls to see how often there is an attempt to hack your PC. The scary news is if you are online for more than half an hour you will be attacked.

Q. How long does it take for a virus solution to be found?

A. Antivirus companies usually know about a virus before it becomes a problem. They have a computer with artificial intelligence that can identify a problem and come up with an answer faster than humans can, this can be less than an hour but can also be measured in minutes.

Q. How many viruses exist today?

A. Viruses are introduced every day, and there are currently well over 62,000 in existence (source: McAfee AVERT Virus Information Library). Compare this with the following statistics (all estimates) and you will see how rampant they have become. In 1990 there were between 200 and 500 in existence, 1991 there were 600–1,000 and in 1992 there were between 1,000–2,300. By 1996, the figure had reached over 10,000 and by 1998 it was well over 20,000. By the turn of the millennium, the figure had reached an amazing 50,000.

While virus numbers are on the increase, the detection of the blighters is ever improving. Remember, a virus created 6 months ago will have been detected and dealt with by today's antivirus software without too many problems. We're going to be looking at some of the best antivirus programs on the market, highlighting some simple protection methods and looking at what are the top five antivirus packages and firewalls. Firewalls are simply security systems which prevent hackers from carrying out their nefarious deeds on your personal computer.

In the fight against viruses, it's always a battle to stay one step ahead of the game. New viruses are being created and introduced everyday, so no matter how good your antivirus software is, and how often it is updated, it can never be 100% effective.

Antivirus manufacturers are well aware of this and it is a constant battle for them to keep up-to-date. An antivirus company can only combat viruses when they come into existence, and not before. If their software does not detect the new virus, then this is where the work begins to create a solution.

Protection methods

Protecting your system, whether you are using a broadband connection or a dial-up, is very much the same. A broadband connection is 'always on', giving the ideal opportunity for hackers and viruses to attack.

The difference is that a broadband connection has a permanent IP address, while a dial-up connection is issued a new IP address each time you log on. This makes the broadband PC more vulnerable, but protecting yourself is still very much the same process. A combination of an IDS (Intrusion Detection System), a firewall and some good antivirus software is the key. Also, simple computing practices can go a long way. Never open any unrecognised emails or attachments and make sure to apply any patches or updates.

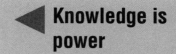

Knowledge is power

Did you know?

The WildList (www.wildlist.org) is an organisation founded by antivirus expert Joe Wells, who has been collecting reports of viruses which have been found spreading in the real world. This list available to the public, free of charge.

Identifying a virus ▶

Virus epidemics are now prime-time news. Nearly every week something is reported about a new 'deadly' virus, worm or Trojan that is wreaking worldwide havoc. What do you do when a virus attacks your PC? Well, if you are running a program like Goback you could simply reset your PC to a point before you had the virus. However, for most people this will not be an option. In this case the most important thing is 'identification', which virus do you have? To find out you are going to need the professionals. You have several options. You can search antivirus companies' knowledge-bases looking for a known virus that matches your computer's symptoms. You could also update your virus software virus definitions and run a virus scan, or use an online virus scanner.

Once you or your antivirus program has identified the possible source of your problem, such as the name and version of the virus, you can begin your defensive assault.

The first stop you should make is at Symantec's Security Response website at http://securityresponse.symantec.com/. This site has the answers and tools you'll need to recover from infection. However, some viruses like the recent Blaster worm may have rendered your computer inoperable, so what then? Well, the answer is simple. You can either spend lots of money finding a technician to do the job, or you could take yourself down to your local library or internet café and use one of their machines to download the remedy. All you will need is a few floppy disks. This is because most support solutions and removal tools available are very small in size (normally around 150 Kb) and will easily fit on a floppy disk.

Once on the Symantec Security Response website, if you have the name and version information of the possible virus, worm or Trojan on your system, you can search the website for the required removal tool or procedure. You can do this by using the search facility or by navigating through the alphabetical list of removal tools. Once found, click on the link and it will take you to a complete support solution for the virus on your system. If the support solution found is a removal tool, the information contained within the support solution will state what virus type and variations will be removed and other virus information. This information includes important notes about the virus on your system, what the removal tool does and removal prerequisites and procedures.

If the support solution supplied is a removal process, including DOS, BOOT and BIOS procedures, the information provided within the support solution will be full and comprehensive. This includes all information about the virus, its payloads and any variation or extended version and its payloads. The removal process will probably be complex but very simple to follow and will probably require at least a restart or two, so for this reason, use the 'Printer Friendly' version link and print out the document for you to follow.

On occasions, especially in the case of worms like Blaster, other support tools may be needed. This is also normally supplied in the Important Information in the Symantec Security Response support solution and direct links are normally provided for you to use. For example, in Blaster's case the Important Information informed the user that the worm exploited a Windows service. This required a patch to be applied to the Windows operating system before starting the removal, but this was small and fitted easily on a floppy disk.

Jargon buster

Worm – a malicious program that uses network communications to spread to multiple computers. Worms commonly use your email service and send themselves to email addresses within your contacts and other email folders. For this reason, always keep an eye on your sent items folder, and try putting a spoof address at the beginning of your contacts list.

Trojan – just about the worst type of malicious program, because its sole purpose is to deliver a package. They can masquerade in many forms, but are commonly created within another fully functional program. When you are running a new third-party software package and your firewall asks you questions regarding permission for internet or network traffic, the chances are high that a Trojan is to blame.

In most circumstances, it is a good idea to disconnect your network and internet cables before you do anything else. This will eliminate the chances of the virus spreading to another computer on your network or utilising your internet connection to spread via email and so on.

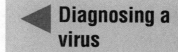

Diagnosing a virus

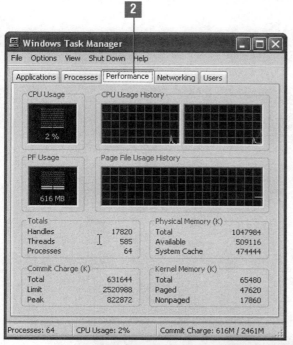

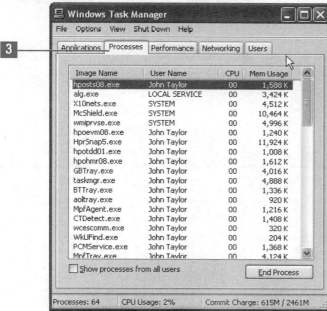

1 If programs are taking a long time to start, take note of which ones. So if Microsoft Word is taking a long time to load, it may be because of a macro virus. These are common but can be stopped by disabling macros from a Microsoft office application.

2 If your computer is running sluggishly, check the CPU and memory usage levels. You can easily check these by looking at the Performance tab from within the Windows Task Manager. Press the Ctrl+Alt+Del keys to start.

3 If the CPU load is high or the amount of free memory is low, check the Processes tab in Task Manager. Look for and note any unusual processes and also look for any high CPU loads and note those processes as well.

4 If you are experiencing unusual and unexpected pop-ups or messages, take a screenshot of these by pressing the Prt Scr (Print Screen) button on your keyboard. Then open Microsoft Paint, paste the image (Ctrl+V) and save it to a folder.

5 If files or folders have disappeared or changed, try using the Windows Search tool and specifying a search for recently updated or altered files and folders. Choose your criteria, when it was modified, the size, file type and even where to look.

12

Diagnosing a virus (cont.)

6 Using Windows Event Viewer (open Run and type 'eventvwr' then press enter) is an easy way to check system errors, messages and warnings over a period of time. It logs all system and file activity, and also logs all system registry activity.

7 If finding information about the possible virus, worm or Trojan on your system is proving difficult; the free Symantec Security Check could be your answer. Just download a small client plug-in and your system will be checked for security threats.

8 Once you have collected all the information you can on what's affecting your system, the final step is to use the Symantec Security Response website. This site is literally the one-stop-shop for information and recovery tools.

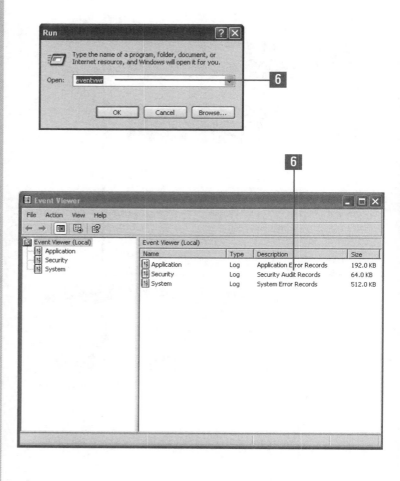

Give your computer a health check using free tools that require nothing more than a web browser and an internet connection. A virus scanner is an essential tool if you use the internet, because this is where you are most likely to catch a nasty infection. It used to be through swapping floppy disks, but now instead virus writers send their spawn through the net.

You can be infected through attachments to emails, or by downloading and running software that websites trick you into accepting. Once you have a virus, getting rid of it isn't easy.

You should have antivirus software installed, but while this provides a good degree of protection, it's only as good as the last update. New viruses appear monthly, and your old virus software may not detect them. Either we get too complacent or are worried about the cost, leaving gaps in security.

You should regularly use an online virus scanner, whether you already have one or not. No single program detects all viruses – it's the one that slips though the net that causes damage, so an online scanner can act as a backup that costs nothing.

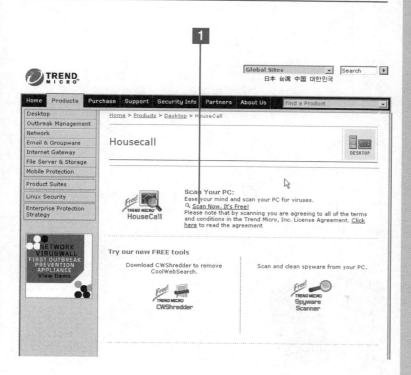

1 Trend Micro's online virus scanner can be found at: http:// housecall.trendmicro.com. You are prompted to enter your email address, but this isn't compulsory, so just ignore it and click the link 'scan without registering'.

2 You are prompted to select your geographic location and a security warning appears. Normally, you should be suspicious of programs that try to install on your computer, but in this case it is okay.

3 When the software has downloaded, you can select the drives to scan. If you don't want to scan a whole drive, click the plus symbol next to it and select a folder. Tick the Auto Clean box and then click Scan.

4 It takes a long time to scan a large hard disk, so go and have a cup of tea while the program works. When it has finished, you should see a message saying that no viruses were found. Well, fingers crossed!

12

Using online virus scanners (cont.)

Panda ActiveScan

1 Go to www.pandasoftware.com/activescan for Panda ActiveScan and click the Scan your PC button in the middle of the page at the bottom. A new window opens, welcoming you to ActiveScan. Click the Scan Now button.

2 Enter your email address on the next page and select the country and the region. Click the Scan Now button.

3 Several files are downloaded to your computer from the Panda website. If any messages appear asking if this is OK, click the Yes button. After a short while a menu screen will appear.

4 Select the options you require, such as the one to automatically disinfect any viruses, then click the item you want to scan, for example, All My Computer or My Documents.

5 Hopefully, you will not see any virus warning windows and you will see a summary on the screen once your entire computer has been scanned. It shows any infections and whether they were disinfected.

6 The Scan Report screen shows any viruses that were detected on your computer, the location and status. If nothing is found, you will not see this screen at all. Close the window to exit ActiveScan.

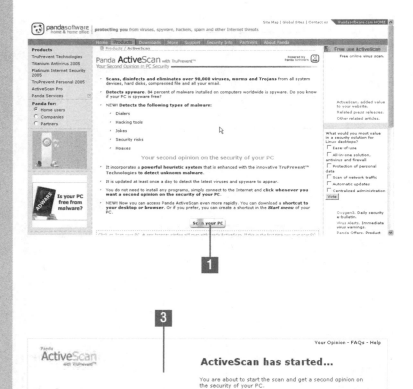

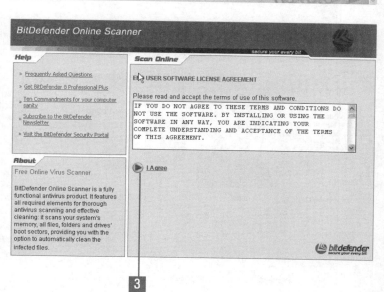

Symantec scans

1 Go to www.symantec.com/securitycheck and you are offered two different types of checks. Security Scan tests whether you are at risk from internet hackers. You should select the Virus Detection option.

2 As with the other scanners, software is downloaded to your computer and you will see several security warning boxes. When downloading is complete, the scanner then analyses the hard disk/drive.

BitDefender scan

3 You are well on your way to becoming an expert at using online virus scanners. Go to www.bitdefender.com/scan/licence.php, click I Agree, and then accept the installation of the scanning software.

4 This time you should scan your email to make sure that nobody has sent you any nasty viral attachments. Tick the option in the list on the left, then tick My Documents and click Start Scanning.

12

Using online virus scanners (cont.)

Kapersky scan

1 If you suspect that a particular file on the hard disk or a CD is infected with a virus, then head on over to http://www.kaspersky.com/virusscanner.

2 Click the Browse button and select the file you want to scan.

3 Click the Online Scanner button, and then wait while the file is uploaded to the website. This can take a few minutes with a slow modem. A report is displayed at the bottom of the page.

MacAfee online

4 There are many more online virus scanners than the ones covered here. Try McAfee's at www.mcafee.com/myapps/mfs/default.asp. McAfee is one of the best-known producers of antivirus software, so you can bet that its online scanner is top notch.

For your information

Online virus scanners work brilliantly with broadband internet connections. The scanner is downloaded and installed in seconds, which means that you can scan your computer as often as you like, checking it every day when you switch on or before you shut down.

Try http://www.ravantivirus.com/scan/

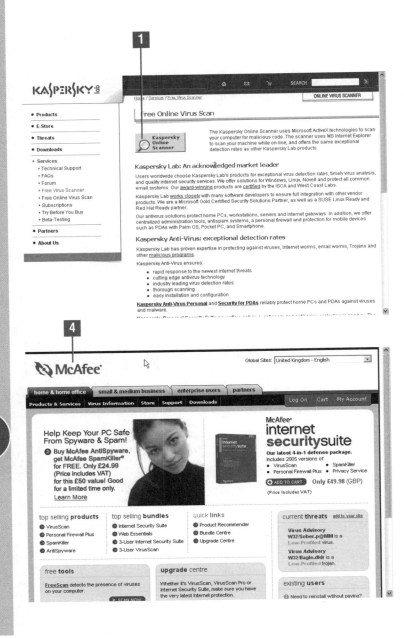

134

The fact that nine out of ten computers contain spyware is an indication of the tenacity of this type of malware, which will exploit the slightest chink in computer defences to infect systems. For this reason, only the best protection will do.

The basis for effective protection against spyware is the use of an appropriate technological solution, integrating reactive and proactive technologies. Nevertheless, users' habits when using computers and the internet have a direct influence on the chances of a system becoming infected by spyware. With this in mind, the following practical tips are designed to help users drastically reduce the chances of their computers being infected by this type of malware.

1 As a lot of spyware enters computers by exploiting software vulnerabilities, it is important to install the latest security patches supplied by software vendors.

2 Carefully read the user licenses of each program that you install on your computer, in particular freeware and shareware versions. Very often, these types of programs install some kind of spyware on the system (in return for using the application).

3 Take care when entering addresses in your browser. Some spyware creators are using web pages, specially designed to download spyware, with domain names similar to those of other famous sites (google.com is just one recent example). The aim is of course, to take advantage of simple user typing errors to install spyware on their systems.

4 Don't download pirate programs, music, films, etc. Regardless of any legal questions, these types of files are a rich source of all types of malware, including spyware.

5 Stay away from underground sites (those related to illegal downloads, hacking tools and techniques, etc.). Not only are these pages often designed to download spyware automatically, but they may also contain applications which, when installed, can drop all types of malware onto systems.

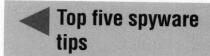

Top five spyware tips

Jargon buster

Broadband – traditionally the name given to a service which uses a single wire to carry many signals, for example cable telephone services that also provide television. Recently it has been applied to fast internet connections though ISPs will call anything from 256k upwards broadband when many don't believe that is true broadband as it's not fast enough. Most broadband connections now are at least 512k.

Malware – a catch-all term for software installed by stealth onto a PC for malevolent purposes (hence the name).

Spyware – applications that monitor your computer and return data about your activities to the people or person's who created them. Often combined with adware. Many spyware applications are malicious, intrusive and incredibly stubborn, proving extremely difficult to remove once they're into your system. In many cases, there's a thin line between spyware and virus.

Upload – the process of transferring one or more files from your computer to one on the internet. Some scanners expect you to upload a file to check it.

12

Learning about well-known viruses

There is now an extraordinary amount of activity from all types of malicious programs. It appears that the latest trend followed by malware creators consists of infesting cyberspace with as many different programs as possible, rather than attempting to cause massive propagation by just one.

Panda Software recently drew up the following ranking for the malware that has emerged recently:

- The rudest. This 'honour' unquestionably goes to Cisum.A. This worm, not satisfied with disabling the anti-malware protection systems in all the PC's it infects, leaves the user the message, 'You're an idiot'. This appears not only in a small window that opens up on the screen, but also blasts from the PC speakers every 5 seconds.

- The most callous. The Zar.A worm fully deserves this 'accolade', as it used the subject of donations to victims of the Asian Tsunami in order to trick users into opening the file containing the malicious code.

- The sexiest. In its own way, the Bropia.E worm – which propagates through instant messenger services – may be considered the sexiest malware to date in 2005. The truth is, that is the only term we can think of for the image in its attachment; a chicken with bikini marks on its body, bronzed, we imagine, by the sun... or by the oven it has just come from.

- The most dangerous. In this case, the choice was quite easy. The winner is Whiter.F, a 'friendly' little malicious program that deletes the content of the entire hard disk. A curious aspect of this malware is that before deleting, it replaces all the user's files with files that contain the following text, 'You did a piracy, you deserve it'.

- The avenging worms. Two malicious programs are neck-in-neck for this prize: on the one hand, the already renowned Trojan Whiter.F and, on the other, the Nopir.A worm. The latter deletes all the files it finds in the computer with COM and MP3 extensions, in addition to reproducing through P2P file-sharing networks. When it attacks a system, it shows an image condemning computer piracy. In any event, don't be taken in: the bit about piracy is just a vulgar excuse to put dangerous malware into circulation.

- The most persistent. Over 4,200 variants launched in 2005 leave no room for doubt: the creators of the Gaobot worms are definitely the most persistent we have seen up to now. The author(s)' intention in launching one variation after another to see if any of them cause an epidemic – always failing – may seem funny, but nothing is farther from the truth. The goal of the Gaobot creators is to put the maximum number of variations into circulation, so that the likelihood of users coming into contact with one of them is as great as possible.

- The most 'socially-minded'. 'Socially-minded' must go between quotation marks, as the Gaobot.IUF and Prex.AM worms are most certainly not envisaged to help the needy, or anything of the sort. Their 'social-mindedness' is limited exclusively to themselves, as what they do is share

Jargon buster

Adware – installed along with other applications and delivers adverts, sometimes through the application window and sometimes through pop-up windows. Often Adware is more of an annoyance than a genuine threat, as many free programs use it to bring in money.

the work when undertaking malicious actions in the PC's where they install themselves. While Gaobot creates a backdoor in the computer that allows hacker attacks, Prex.AM takes charge of sending false messages by instant messenger so that other users download the file that contains both malicious programs.

- **The most enticing.** This award goes to the V variation of the extensive Sober family of worms. The lure of free tickets for the Soccer World Cup to be held in Germany in 2006 allowed it to reach a significant level of propagation. Fortunately, users are a bit more savvy now and the creator was unsuccessful in his objective of causing a new epidemic.

- **The extortionist.** It appears that asking for money in exchange for release from the actions of malicious program is now coming into vogue as a new form of online fraud. The highlights of this section are the PGPCoder Trojans that encrypt files on the hard disk and demand money or the purchase of certain applications to be able to decipher them. It is somewhat similar to what other malware, such as SpywareNo does; this one also requires the purchase of a particular anti-spyware software in order to get rid of it.

- **The most versatile.** Eyeveg.D is one of those impossible-to-classify types of malware. It has certain characteristics of Trojans and backdoor, all for the purpose of stealing confidential data from the PC's it affects and allowing in remote attacks. For even greater effectiveness, it can reproduce through email. What a pity that all that genius is wasted on malicious activities!

- **The bank robbers.** More than banks, what this malware attempts to do is to empty out users' bank accounts. The multiple variations of the Bancos family of Trojans all have the same ultimate goal: to get users' data in order to perpetrate all types of financial fraud.

12

Removing spyware

If you spend any time online at all – and especially if you download files from the internet – spyware is something you really have to worry about. For those not familiar with these unsavoury little characters, they really are the bane of all net users' lives; the chances are that there is some form of spyware lurking on your PC right now. In a nutshell, they are little files, often remotely executable programs that enter your system on the back of files you download or in internet cookies picked up from sites you visit. They don't pose any real threat, but they will cause things like pop-up ads (nobody likes those) and in extreme cases hijack your browser to guide you to the sites they want you to visit. Essentially, it's a form of guerrilla advertising and market research. A lot of spyware can log the sites you visit, and even the key presses you make, then send them back to a host elsewhere on the net. Fortunately, you are about to meet Ad-Aware; its sole purpose is to kill unwanted pests on your system by scanning your drives and picking up the little critters before they get the chance to do any harm. Follow these simple tips to rid your system of spyware and allow faster and pop-up free web browsing.

Start Ad-Aware se

1 Here is the screen you will be presented with on running Ad-Aware se. As you can see there are a number of buttons to choose from, each allowing you different options within the program.

2 The most important is the Scan now button – go ahead and click.

Prepare for scanning

3 Next is the scan preparation screen which allows you to set the details of your system scan.

4 It is probably easiest to click Next, but if there are only selected folders you wish to scan or you're strapped for time, there are alternative options.

5 Click Next.

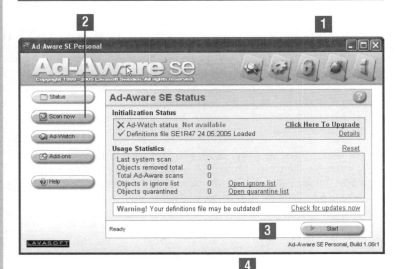

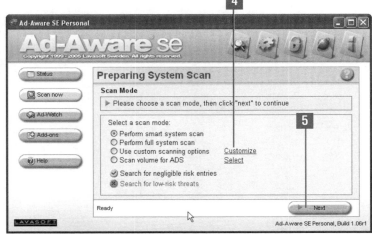

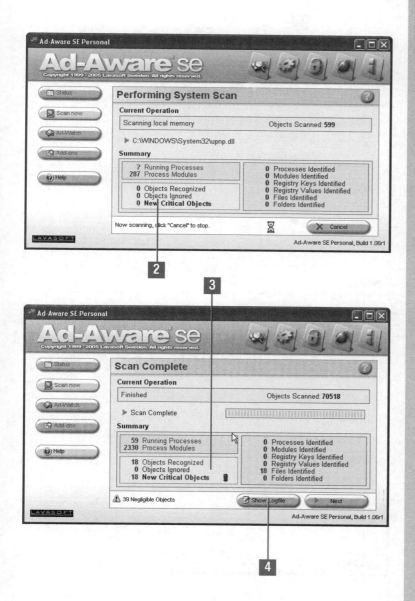

Scan in progress

1 Depending on the options you chose previously your system will be scanned for all signs of pests.

2 This may take a long time if you have a larger hard drive, but it's well worth it. As the scan takes place you can watch how many items of spyware have been found so far.

Scan is finished

3 Once the scan is complete the number of suspected files found is listed and you are given the option to view those suspected.

4 Click the Show Logfile button to see the list and any information on the files found. This is important to determine exactly where the file is located and hopefully gain information on where it may have come from.

12

Removing spyware (cont.)

What have we found?

1 This will display a report listing all spyware references.

2 Click on the Critical Objects tab.

File quarantine or removal

3 A list of the files found is now displayed which will let you choose which one you wish to deal with.

4 Right-click in the box next to the file you want to select. This will place a green tick in the box. You can select or deselect all the files in preparation to take action.

5 You can now choose to quarantine or remove the files selected. Quarantining a file will mean it is disabled but can be restored when required. If you choose to remove the file then it will be permanently deleted.

6 If you click Quarantine you will be asked to enter a name for the selected files, which will remind you what and where they are later. On confirmation you will be asked if you are sure you want to quarantine these files.

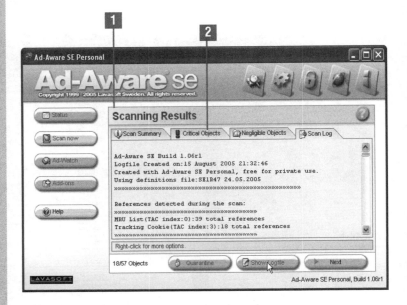

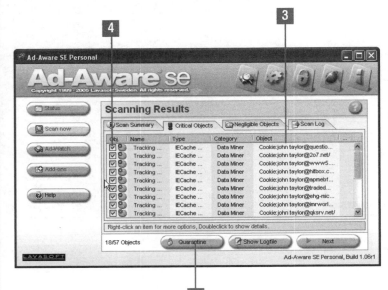

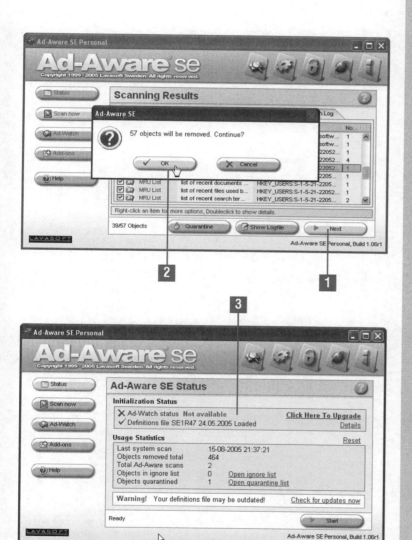

Delete files

1 To remove a file for good, simply select the files required and click Next.

2 You will be asked if you are sure you want to delete this file. Click OK.

Finish up

3 With the items successfully removed or quarantined, Ad-Aware will now give you a helpful screen listing of all the actions taken. It's a useful document for making sure you don't continue to get plagued by this sort of thing and for enabling files you have quarantined but wish to restore.

For your information

While Ad-Aware can provide an excellent service for removing rogue files from your system, spyware advances every day and new styles are created with alarming regularity, so you constantly need to update your program to recognise and tackle the new and improved bandits that crop up.

12

Data recovery

Introduction

We have all done it, lost track of a file or even a whole set of files. There are several reasons why you might lose a file. The first is that you don't know where files are saved by the program you are using. The second is the file was not saved where you expected it to be, or you just plain forgot where you saved it.

Another reason is that you deleted a file or set of files that you didn't mean to. You would think that you would never do that, but the day will come when you do! It's then that you will be glad of a second chance. The time might come when files you deleted, because you thought you no longer needed them, suddenly become vital, but because you thought you did not need them, you cleaned out the Recycle Bin and they are well and truly gone.

Well, actually, they are not gone, the file is still on your hard drive and can be recovered with specialist software. This is what has surprised so many famous people who thought they had wiped all the files off their computer.

In this section you will be shown how to use Search to find lost files, how to recover deleted files from the Recycle Bin, how to use a commercial file rescue program to restore dead files and how to restore from backed up files.

What you'll do

Find lost files

Use the Recycle Bin

Undelete files

Rescue photos, etc.

Use your backup

Finding lost files

The best way to track down missing or lost files is to call on the help of a Windows XP applet called Search. Search is a very powerful tool that can look for missing files. The Search Wizard can be configured to look in every drive on your system and your network. This is a sure way of finding your missing file but may take a long time. If you can remember which drive you saved to, you can ask Search to only look at that drive, making a search considerably quicker.

Start to Search

1 Open the Start menu and click Search in the second column.

2 At the Search window, you need to decide what you want to search for. You can ask Search to look for certain file types, so if you have lost your favourite music file you can instruct Search to look for pictures, music and video files only, which again saves time.

3 On the left hand side of the screen you will see a small dog and a speech bubble menu.

4 Next select the type of search. In this case, we are looking for a lost file so want the most exhaustive search. Click on All files and folders.

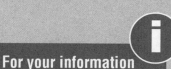

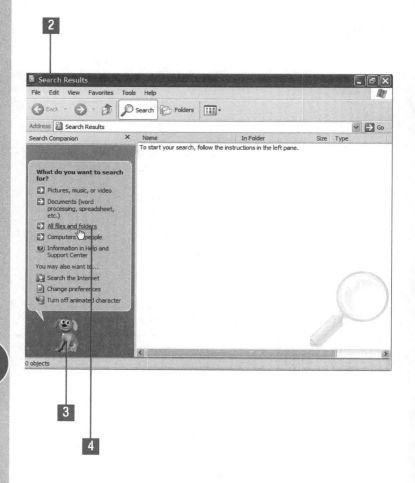

For your information

To find a missing file you have to know the file name, don't you? No, actually you don't, you can type in part of a name, for example, 'my' or 'file' for a word document called myfile.doc. You don't even need to know the file name as Search can look inside documents to find matching words or phrases, for example, find all files with 'the quick brown fox' in the text.

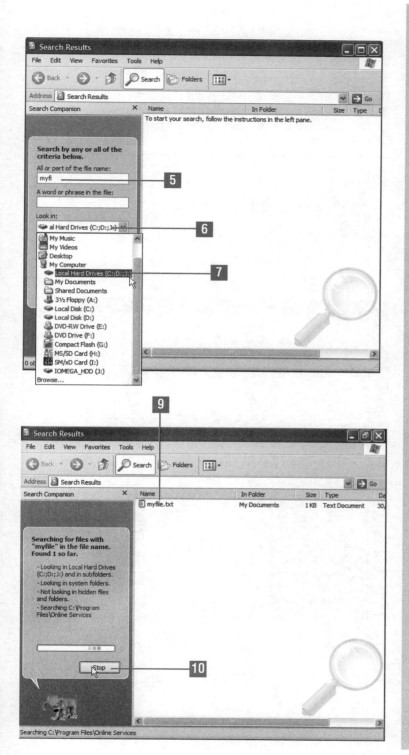

5 The menu now changes to the search criteria menu. Click into the All or part of name box and type in as much of the file name as you can remember.

6 You can select where you want to search for the file. Search will give you a default selection of all local drives, which is usually the best to pick.

7 If you want to look in a specific place click on the down arrow to the right of the Look in box and select from the list of choices.

8 Click Search. Search Companion (the little dog) will start working through your drives looking for your file.

9 Any matches will be displayed in the panel to the right. This panel is divided into four columns called Name, In folder, Size and Type. This should be enough information for you to confirm which is your lost file.

10 If your file is found quickly, but the Search Companion carries on searching the rest of your drives then click Stop to suspend the search.

Did you know?

You could end up with a long list of possibilities for your lost file and using the date column will help you narrow down which is the right file.

Using the Recycle Bin

For the most part, as long as your files are well ordered and you are not running out of hard disk space, it's not a good idea to delete any file. However, if you need to find extra space then deleting files may be the only option. What happens if you delete a file only to find that you needed that file! When you delete a file it's not gone – you have a second and third chance to get it back.

The second chance is to use the Recycle Bin to get your file back. All deleted files are stored in the bin just in case you need them. Be warned that they don't stay there forever. If you empty the bin you lose the chance to get your file back this way.

1 The Recycle Bin can be found on the main desktop. It's the icon that looks like a waste paper bin. Double-click on the icon to open the bin.

2 The Recycle Bin window shows the deleted files on the right hand side.

3 The Recycle Bin tasks are on the left side.

4 Emptying the Recycle Bin is definitely **not** what we want to do.

5 The Restore all items task will move all the deleted files back to their original position.

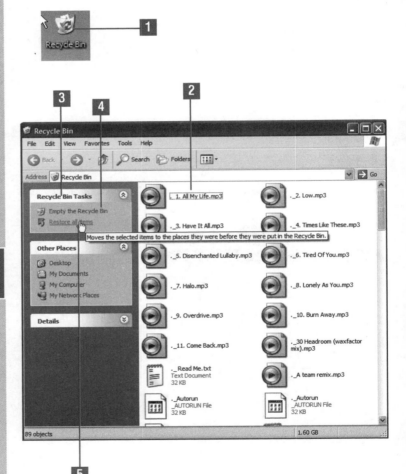

Jargon buster

Recycle Bin – a folder linked to an icon on the Windows Desktop where you can drag folders or files that you want to delete. When you put items into the Recycle Bin, they are not permanently deleted, and can be easily recovered by double-clicking on the Bin icon, and restoring them back to their original folders. To permanently delete a file, you need to empty the Recycle Bin.

Restore files from the bin

1 You can also pull files one at a time out of the Recycle Bin. Right-click on the file you want to restore. This brings up a context menu.

2 At the top of the menu is the Restore option. Click this option and the file will be put back to its original position on your drive.

1

2

Recycle Bin

File   Edit   View   Favorites   Tools   Help

Back   Search   Folders

Address   Recycle Bin   Go

Recycle Bin Tasks

Empty the Recycle Bin

Restore this item

Other Places

Desktop

My Documents

My Computer

My Network Places

Details

HP Director
Shortcut
4 KB

HP Photo & Imaging
Shortcut
4 KB

._30 Headroom (waxfactor mix).mp3

| Restore |
| Cut |
| Delete |
| **Properties** |

._A team remix.mp3

._Bombo.

._Camtasia 1.0.1
1 File
32 KB

._Demon Days.mp3

._Dirty Harry.mp3

._Don't Get Lost In Heaven.mp3

._El Manana.mp3

._Every Planet We Reach Is De.mp3

._Feel Good Inc..mp3

._Fire Coming Out Of The Monk.mp3

._heads.mp3

._HyperSnap3.exe

._Intro.mp3

Original Location: J:\Documents\MP3\7-7-05 Type: MP3 Format Sound Size: 32.0 KB   32.0 KB

Did you know?

The Recycle Bin tells you if it's empty or if it has files inside. The icon changes from an empty bin to a full bin.

Recycle Bin

Bin full

Recycle Bin

Bin empty

Undeleting files

If you empty your Recycle Bin you might be forgiven for thinking that your files are now deleted and lost forever! Don't panic, they're not, but you will need a specialised piece of software to recover them.

Use iolo Search and Recover

 The Search and Recover main menu has many options.

 You need the File Rescue Wizard. Click on the magic hat icon.

For your information

This example uses Search and Recover, a commercial program available from www.iolo.com, but of course there are other programs available.

Important

It's a very good idea not to write any more data to the drive with your deleted files on until you undelete it. This is because Windows will eventually overwrite files marked for deletion. You might be very unlucky and Windows decides to overwrite your file. At that point you won't be able to get it back.

Narrow down your search

3 The first menu is the Things to Search for menu. You can select to search for all files, but the wizard will come back with a very big list depending on how long you have had your PC and how many files you and XP have deleted.

4 If you know what type of file you are looking for it's a good idea to narrow down the search. If you have lost a document select the tick next to the Documents option. You can select more than one option by placing a tick in the box.

5 Click Next to move on to the Places to Look menu.

Rescue photos, etc.

6 You can look for files on devices not permanently connected to your PC. Click here to find out more.

7 Select which drives you want to include in your search. To search the C: drive select the tick box next to local drive.

8 Click Scan.

Did you know?

If your PC has more than one drive you can select each of them in turn or all together.

Undeleting files (cont.)

Find files

9 The wizard will now search for all deleted files in your chosen locations. A progress bar is displayed while it's searching.

10 A list of files found is displayed.

11 You have several choices, e.g. you can preview a file. This is useful for text files but not much else.

12 Select the file you want to recover, it will be highlighted in blue.

13 Click Recover to undelete the file.

Did you know?

You can rescue files from removable media such as digital camera memory cards. It is possible to delete files using the camera but it's all too easy to delete the wrong one! You can get it back using the Search and Rescue program, but remember don't take any more pictures as you might overwrite the deleted image. Best to use a new card until you have sorted out the problem.

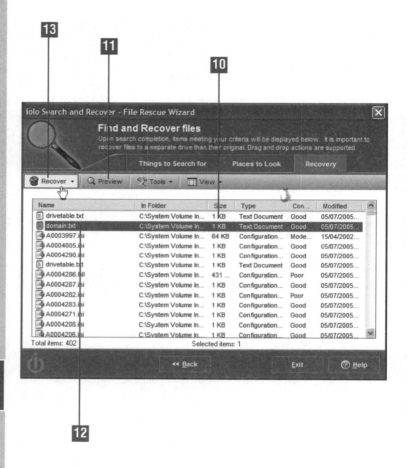

Select files

14 Now select where you want to put the restored file. You can browse your PC to find the best place.

15 When you're done, select the Exit button.

Important

It is important to recover your files to a separate drive, other than the original, if you are recovering more than one file. As explained before, this file could overwrite one of your other files.

Using your backup

Hopefully you made a backup earlier in the book using the Microsoft Backup tool. Restoring a backup is the simplest way of restoring a deleted file. First you need to locate your Backup, on your hard drive, floppy disks, tape, etc. You can restore whole sections of your drive or individual files.

Use Backup Wizard

1 Backup is located on the System Tools menu. Open the Start menu, point to All Programs, then Accessories, then System Tools.

2 Click Backup to start the program.

3 Backup starts in friendly mode as a wizard. To opt to use the wizard, click Next.

Restore files

4 This menu allows you to backup files or restore them from your backup file.

5 Select the Restore option by clicking the radio button.

6 Click Next to move on.

Did you know?

There is a second advanced option but the wizard is much friendlier and will get the job done.

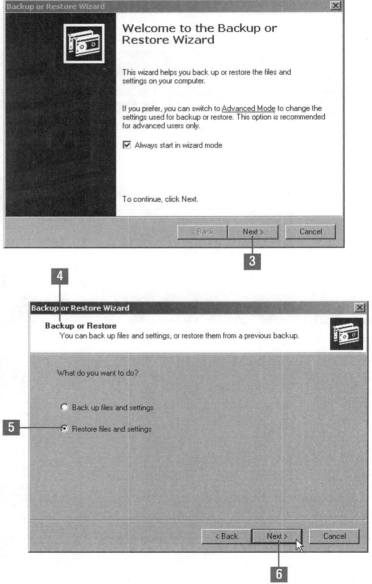

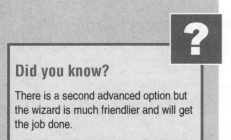

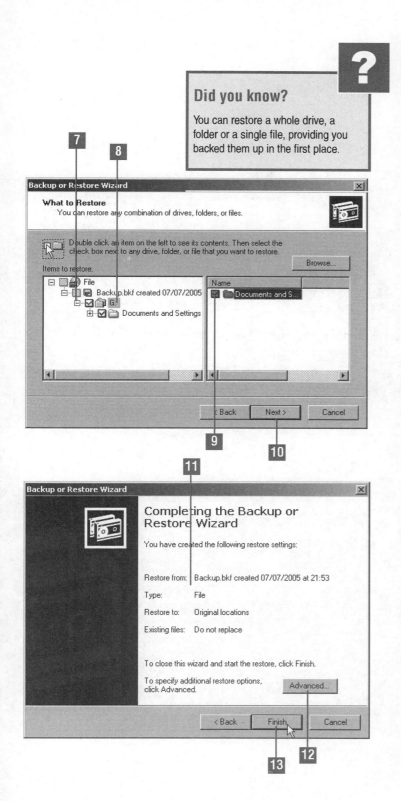

Did you know?

You can restore a whole drive, a folder or a single file, providing you backed them up in the first place.

Select items

7 You need to select the files to restore. Click on the plus signs to open locations so you can see what is inside.

8 You can double-click on any item to see its contents.

9 Select the check box next to the item or items you want to restore.

10 Click Next to start Restore.

11 This menu is a summary of what will happen next; in this case one file will be restored to its original position. As a safety feature the wizard will not overwrite or replace a file if it is already there.

12 The Advanced button lets you change settings such as allowing overwriting.

13 Click Finish to continue.

Did you know?

Restore is set to not overwrite existing files as it is highly likely that the existing file is the most up-to-date file. This is because your file was backed up in the past and you may have worked on it since. If you restored the old file you would lose the new work.

Using your backup (cont.)

Follow progress

1 The wizard will now display a progress dialog box. This has useful information.

2 The first box tells us which drive the information is coming from.

3 The Label box tells us when the backup was created.

4 The Status box tells us what the wizard is doing now.

5 The Progress box tells us how much is done and how much is left.

6 As a large backup can take a long time, the time box is particularly useful as it not only tells you how long the task has taken so far, but also an estimate of how long is left.

7 The Processing box tells you which file is currently being restored, how big the file is and progress of the current restoration.

8 You can cancel the Restore at this point by clicking Cancel at the top of the menu.

9 Once the backup is complete the wizard lets you know. A new button is displayed. Click Report to generate a report.

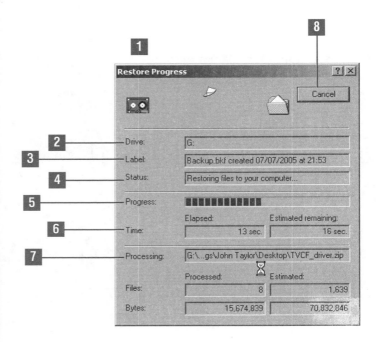

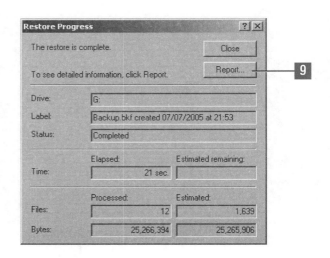

10

```
backup02 - Notepad                                      _ □ ×
File  Edit  Format  View  Help
Restore Status
Operation: Restore

Backup of "G:", Restored to"G: "
Backup set #1 on media #1
Backup description: "Set created 07/07/2005 at 21:53"

Restore started on 08/07/2005 at 06:01.
Restore completed on 08/07/2005 at 06:01.
Directories: 194
Files: 12
Bytes: 25,266,394
Time:   21 seconds

----------------------
```

Read the report

10 The report is generated as a text file. You will need to open it in a text editor such as Notepad to read it.

For your information

It can be useful to keep these reports so you have a record of what you have done, which files you have restored and when.

Important

Always store your backups on good quality media. You don't want your backup to fail because it's on cheap media.

The keyboard

Introduction

The QWERTY keyboard was developed in 1868 and this layout is basically
unchanged and still in use today for computer keyboards. The keyboard along
with the mouse is the main input device used by all computers. The keyboard
allows you to input information and interact with the computer. All computer
keyboards have all the letters of the alphabet, numbers 0–9 and additional
special operational keys.

Keyboards have become more than typewriters, they are now entertainment
control centres. Today's keyboards have moved on from the basic QWERTY
keyboards with the basic keys. All keyboards supplied today are ergonomically
designed to reduce the strain of typing on the fingers. Many keyboards now
feature extra keys and some even have mouse-like controls built into the
keyboard. Some manufacturers have integrated their keyboards with Windows,
providing many keys that directly access frequently used Windows functions.
Some keyboards even have keys you can program yourself.

What you'll do

Use the keyboard

Use Windows XP shortcuts

Using the keyboard ▶

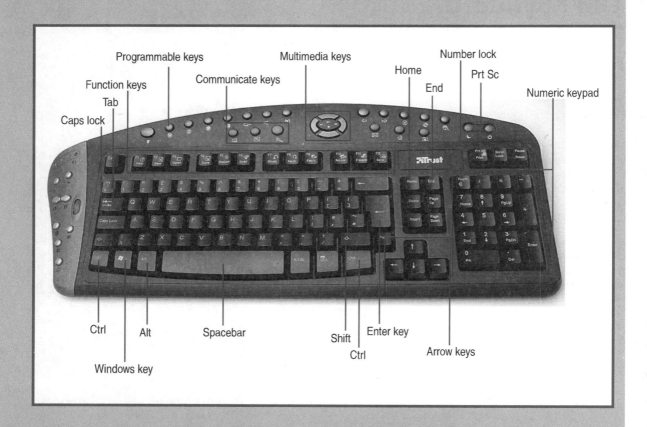

Labels on keyboard diagram:
- Caps lock
- Tab
- Function keys
- Programmable keys
- Communicate keys
- Multimedia keys
- Home
- End
- Number lock
- Prt Sc
- Numeric keypad
- Ctrl
- Alt
- Windows key
- Spacebar
- Shift
- Ctrl
- Enter key
- Arrow keys

Safe cleaning tips

Turn the computer off before cleaning the keyboard.

Don't spray or squirt any type of liquid onto or into your keyboard, always use a damp cloth.

Use a vacuum to suck up any debris stuck between the keys.

Don't use chemicals or household cleaning solvents as some solvents can damage the key top markings.

Never eat or drink around the computer (easier said than done).

Unplug the keyboard and clean spills immediately. Allow plenty of time to dry before using again.

- **Programmable keys** – allow you to program shortcuts to your most used programs.

- **Communicate keys** – one touch buttons allow access to your email and web browser.

- **Multimedia keys** – standard familiar controls allow you to control your music and videos.

- **Windows key** – brings up the Windows Start menu.

- **Function keys** – these have standard functions assigned to them, for example, the F1 key brings up the Help menu for Windows or the program you are using.

- **Enter key** – confirms any entries made, also acts as a line feed.

- **Numeric keypad** – set out like a calculator this section allows easy number entry.

- **Number lock** – turns the numbers on and off.

- **Prt Sc** – previously, this was used to send a copy of the screen to the printer. You can now use it to take a screen shot of the display, pressing this key sends the current screen image to the computer clipboard.

- **Arrow keys** – allow you to navigate up, down, left and right.

- **Ctrl** – short for Control, this key is used in combination with other keys to perform a function. For example, Ctrl+Alt+Del to start Task Manager.

- **Alt** – short for Alternate, this key allows access to extra functions for all keys on the keyboard.

- **Shift** – allows you to type capital letters, and the symbols on the number keys while it's pressed.

- **Caps lock** – locks the keyboard to type only capital letters.

- **Spacebar** – creates an empty space.

- **Tab** – can be used to add an indentation at the beginning of a text line. In a program a tab allows you to move around different parts of a menu, display, or page. Alt and Tab switches between open windows or applications.

- **Home** – returns you to the beginning of the line or the beginning of a document.

- **End** – moves the text cursor to the end of the line, paragraph, page or document.

For your information

Not all keyboards have programmable keys.

Jargon buster

Hot keys – the popularity of the internet has brought about new keyboards with extra buttons, known as hot keys. These allow you to jump to your email or favourite website by pressing a single button. You'll need to make sure you've installed the software that came with your keyboard if you want these hot keys to work.

Using Windows XP shortcuts

Cut & Paste

Ctrl & X = Cut.
Ctrl & V = Paste.
Ctrl & C = Copy.
Ctrl & Z = Undo.

Delete

Del = Delete the selected item.
Shift & Del = Delete permanently without moving the item to the Recycle Bin.

Dragging

Ctrl plus left click of mouse button and hold and drag = Copy the item.

Desktop shortcuts

Ctrl & Shift while dragging an item = Create a shortcut for the selected item.
Alt & Spacebar = Open the shortcut menu for the active window.

Rename

F2 key = Rename the selected item.

Text

Ctrl & left arrow = Move the text insertion point to the start of the previous word.
Ctrl & right arrow = Move the text insertion point to the start of the next word.
Ctrl & down arrow = Move the text insertion point to the start of the next paragraph.
Ctrl & up arrow = Move the text insertion point to the start of the previous paragraph.
Ctrl & Shift with any of the arrow keys = Select and highlight a block of text.
Shift with any of the arrow keys = Select more than one item in a window or on the desktop, or select text in a document.
Ctrl & A = Select all.

Quick start and finish

F3 key = Start Windows Search and look for a files.
Ctrl & Esc = Start the Start menu.
Alt & F4 = Close the active item, or quit the active program.
Ctrl & F4 = Close the active document in programs that enable you to have multiple documents open simultaneously.
Esc = Cancel the current task.

Window navigation

Alt & Tab = Cycle through all open programs or windows.

Alt & Esc = Cycle through items in the order that they had been opened.

F6 key = Cycle through the screen elements in a window or on the desktop.

More information

F1 key = Display Help.

F4 key = Display the items in the active list.

Alt & Enter = Show the properties of the selected object.

F4 key = Display the Address bar list in My Computer or Windows Explorer.

Shift & F10 = Display the shortcut menu for the selected item.

Alt & Spacebar = Show the System menu for the active window.

Program menus

Alt & the Underlined letter in a menu name = Display the corresponding menu.

Underlined letter in a command name on an open menu = Perform the named command.

F10 key = Activate the menu bar in the active program.

Left arrow = Open the next menu to the left, or close a sub-menu.

Right arrow = Open the next menu to the right, or open a sub-menu.

F5 key = Update the active window works for updating web pages as well.

Autoplay

Shift when you insert a CD-ROM into the CD-ROM drive = Prevent the CD-ROM from automatically playing.

Dialog box Windows shortcuts

Ctrl & Tab = Move forward through the tabs.

Ctrl & Shift & Tab = Move backward through the tabs.

Tab= Move forward through the options.

Shift & Tab = Move backward through the options.

Alt & Underlined letter = Perform the corresponding command or select the corresponding option.

Big keys

Enter = Perform the command for the active option or button.

Backspace = View the folder one level up in My Computer or Windows Explorer.

Spacebar = Select or clear the check box if the active option is a check box.

Reinstalling Windows

Introduction

There comes a time in every computer's life when it starts slowing down. Startup times get longer, it may even display a few annoying error messages you just can't get rid of. You assume that these problems are because your PC is getting a bit long in the tooth, but before you bite the bullet and spring for the latest model, you could try a fresh install of Windows. Many of the problems mentioned are nothing to do with the age of your computer, but as you add and remove programs, hardware and updates Windows gets clogged and runs slower.

Think back to when you first got your computer out of the box, you didn't think it was slow then, did you? So why not return your computer to its original state. This will remove all the clutter giving you a fresh start and effectively your new PC back.

In this age of virus, spyware and worm attacks you will have to make sure you use Windows Update to add the security fixes and patches that have been released since your version of Windows was manufactured. These will inevitably slow Windows down again but not to the extent those months of installing and uninstalling can do.

What you'll do

Prepare for a Windows XP reinstall

Use a CD as a boot disk

Install Windows XP

Partition a disk

Prepare the disk

Load Windows XP files

Customize Windows XP

Preparing for Windows XP reinstall

When contemplating a clean install it is important to backup as much information as possible – and a complete backup is recommended. The following task will guide you through the files you must include when you are making copies of your files, some of which are not immediately obvious. Apart from your documents, you should also make copies of your fonts, favourites and cookies, and ensure that you have the installation disks for any applications.

Find the data to backup

1 Documents — this is one of the obvious sets of files to backup. Most users keep their documents in the My Documents folder.

2 It is important you get all of the files. Don't forget that some programs store files in folders created by the program during the install process.

3 You may have created your own folders. Make sure to spend some time tracking them down.

4 Fonts are stored in the Windows directory on the Windows drive. So when this drive is cleared, any fonts you or other programs have added will be lost.

5 Copy all fonts to a new temporary drive.

Timesaver tip

Any files stored on the Desktop are stored on the boot drive, the same drive as Windows and the drive you are going to clear. So make sure you copy these files off the desktop.

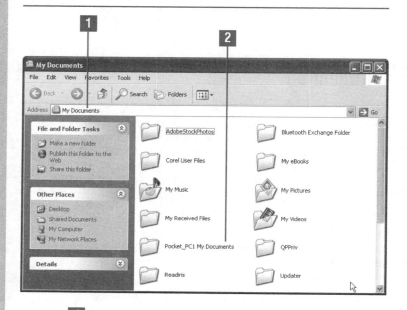

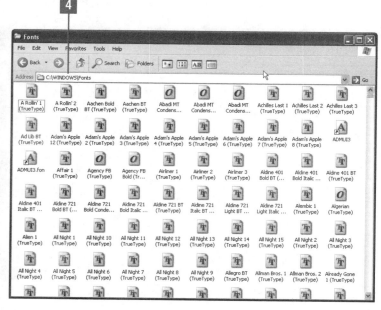

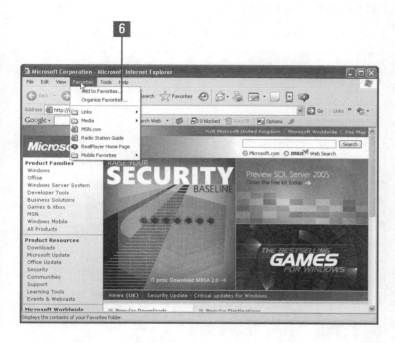

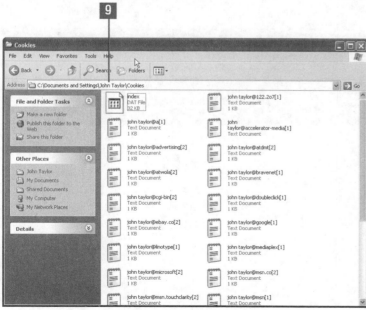

6 If you have been using the internet for a while you will most probably have a large selection of favourite sites. You need to back these up by making a copy.

7 Check to make sure you have the original disks for all programs you have on your computer. Even if the programs are installed to a different drive there is a good chance they will stop working and have to be reinstalled.

8 Make sure you have the original driver disks as you may well have to reinstall the driver for your computer's hardware. Windows will detect and install drivers in most cases.

9 Cookies are not always a bad thing if they are helpful. They can store your username and password so you don't have to log on every time. The problem with this is you tend to forget the password because you never have to type it. So make sure you backup any cookies for these sites.

For your information

Windows XP now has many versions:
Windows XP Home Full
Windows XP Home Upgrade
Windows XP Professional Full
Windows XP Professional Upgrade
Windows XP SP2
Windows Vista (due October 2006)

Using a CD as a boot disk

The Windows XP install disk is also a boot disk, which means it can be used to startup your computer. However, to get your computer to look at the Windows CD-ROM, you first have to change the device on which your computer looks for the boot up files. To do this you need to configure the CMOS and tell it to look for the CD-ROM first.

To start the CMOS setup utility, follow the instructions in Chapter 7.

Set the boot sequence

1 When the CMOS setup utility main menu is displayed, press the down arrow key on your keyboard. This will move the highlight bar to the Advance BIOS Features option. When this option is highlighted press Enter.

2 You now need to change the boot order. Move the highlight bar to select First Boot Device.

3 Press Enter and the First Boot Device Menu will be displayed.

4 Use the up and down arrow keys. As you move them a square will move from box to box.

5 Navigate to the CD-ROM box and press Enter to select. The CD-ROM will now be the first place the PC looks for the files to boot it.

6 Finally press F10 on your keyboard to save the change.

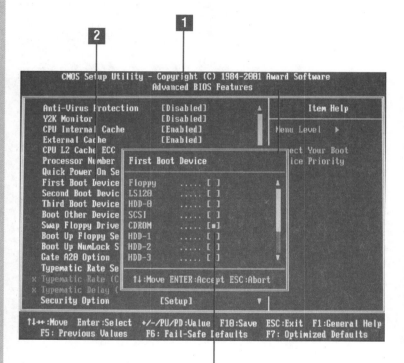

Jargon buster

Boot – switch on and start up the computer and its operating system.

```
Sec. Master Disk  : DVD-RW,PIO 4
Sec. Slave  Disk  : None


Pri. Master Disk  HDD S.M.A.R.T. capability .... Disabled
Pri. Slave  Disk  HDD S.M.A.R.T. capability .... Disabled


PCI device listing ...
Bus No. Device No. Func No. Vendor/Device Class Device Class              IRQ

  8        8        8     8886   1848   8788  Simple COMM. Cntrlr         11
  8       18        8     1182   8882   8481  Multimedia Device           12
  8       18        1     1182   7882   8988  Input Device                NA
  8       12        8     184C   8488   8288  Network Cntrlr              11
  8       17        1     1186   8571   8181  IDE Cntrlr                  14
  1        8        8     1882   4158   8388  Display Cntrlr              NA
  2        8        8     1833   8835   8C83  Serial Bus Cntrlr           11
  2        8        1     1833   8835   8C83  Serial Bus Cntrlr           12
  2        8        2     1833   88E8   8C83  Serial Bus Cntrlr            5
  2       11        8     184C   8828   8C88  Serial Bus Cntrlr           11
                                             ACPI Controller              9
Verifying DMI Pool Data ............
Boot from CD :
Press any key to boot from CD.._
```

8

9

Restart

7 Once the CMOS settings have been saved, the computer will restart using these new settings.

8 A new message is displayed telling you the computer is booting from the CD-ROM.

9 The computer will now ask you to confirm that you want to boot from the CD-ROM by pressing any key on the keyboard.

15

For your information

If you don't press a key, after waiting a few seconds to give you a chance to hit the key, the computer will boot from your hard drive as normal.

Installing Windows XP ▶

Using the Windows install disk as the boot disk will automatically run the setup sequence on your PC. First, Setup will check the configuration of your PC. It will then move on to load the basic files it needs to use the CD-ROM, display and network. Keep an eye on the bottom of the screen, as it will ask you some questions. If you don't answer these questions the Windows Setup program will continue the setup.

1 The Windows Setup program will now start and get ready to install Windows XP on your computer. Before it does it needs to check out your computer and make sure it's compatible and there is enough space to install itself.

2 This message is merely a list, it is not an interactive menu of the sort you are used to. You don't have to highlight or select any choices from the list.

3 As we are installing Windows from scratch you will need to select the first item from the displayed list. To do this, simply press the enter key on the keyboard to continue the installation.

4 The second option is the repair option. You can use this to repair Windows XP and keep all your old settings.

5 This option allows you to back out of the installation if you have changed your mind, or find yourself at this menu unexpectedly.

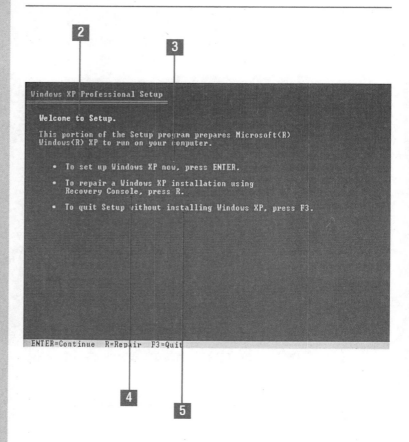

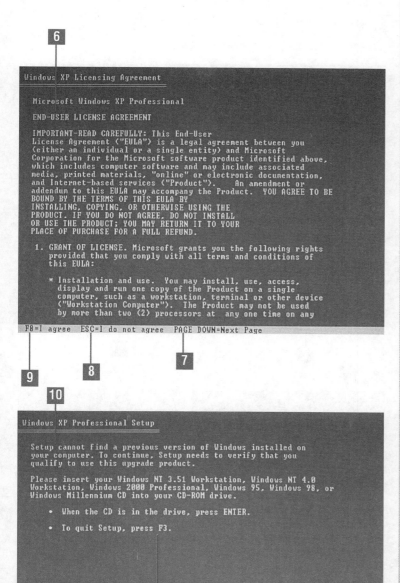

Installing Windows XP (cont.)

The End-user License Agreement

6 The Licensing agreement page is one most users just accept at face value. You should read it at least once.

7 The agreement is many pages long. To get to the next page, press the Page Down key on your keyboard.

8 If you find yourself not agreeing, Microsoft has given you the option of not accepting. Press Esc. You will not be able to continue with the install and you will have to install another operating system such as Linux.

9 As the object of this task is to install Windows press the F8 key to agree.

Message about Windows

10 Most users will not see this message. It depends on what version of Windows you have currently installed and what Windows install disk you are using. We used a Windows XP professional upgrade disk.

11 Because an upgrade disk was used, the Setup program will need to verify there is a full version of Windows. If you have a full version you will need to change the upgrade disk for a full version disk. This full version can be any version of Windows, for example Windows 98.

12 If you don't have a full version you will have to press F3 and quit the install.

15

Partitioning a disk ▶

1 Now comes the drastic bit. You need to wipe out all traces of the old Windows and its settings. This is so drastic it will completely remove the old hard drive partition. You need to select the drive you are going to remove the partition from. Use the up and down arrows on the keyboard to highlight your selection.

2 Now press D to delete the partition. (Final warning – this will remove all information from this disk and you won't be able to get it back.)

Going for it

3 Windows will now warn you of the consequences of the action you are about to perform.

4 To backup and go back to the earlier screen press the Esc key.

5 To continue press the Enter key.

Jargon buster

Partition – A method of dividing a hard drive into multiple virtual drives.

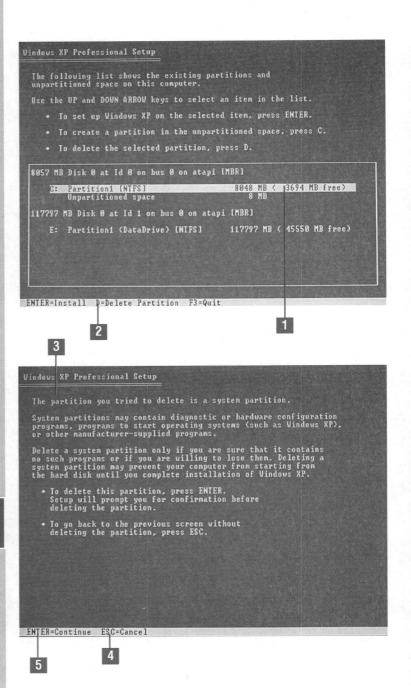

```
Windows XP Professional Setup

 The following list shows the existing partitions and
 unpartitioned space on this computer.

 Use the UP and DOWN ARROW keys to select an item in the list.

    • To set up Windows XP on the selected item, press ENTER.

    • To create a partition in the unpartitioned space, press C.

    • To delete the selected partition, press D.

 8057 MB Disk 0 at Id 0 on bus 0 on atapi [MBR]

     C: Partition1 [NTFS]                8048 MB ( 3694 MB free)
        Unpartitioned space                 8 MB

 117797 MB Disk 0 at Id 1 on bus 0 on atapi [MBR]

     E: Partition1 (DataDrive) [NTFS]   117797 MB ( 45550 MB free)



 ENTER=Install  D=Delete Partition  F3=Quit
```

1 **2**

3

```
Windows XP Professional Setup

 The partition you tried to delete is a system partition.

 System partitions may contain diagnostic or hardware configuration
 programs, programs to start operating systems (such as Windows XP),
 or other manufacturer-supplied programs.

 Delete a system partition only if you are sure that it contains
 no such programs or if you are willing to lose them. Deleting a
 system partition may prevent your computer from starting from
 the hard disk until you complete installation of Windows XP.

    • To delete this partition, press ENTER.
      Setup will prompt you for confirmation before
      deleting the partition.

    • To go back to the previous screen without
      deleting the partition, press ESC.




 ENTER=Continue  ESC=Cancel
```

5 **4**

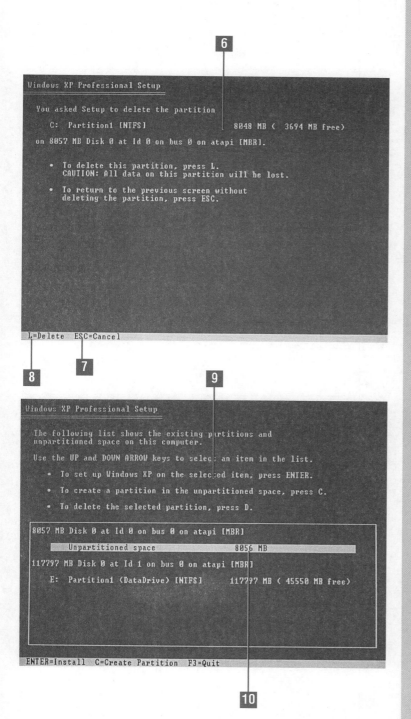

6

Windows XP Professional Setup

You asked Setup to delete the partition

   C: Partition1 [NTFS]   8048 MB (3694 MB free)

on 8057 MB Disk 0 at Id 0 on bus 0 on atapi [MBR].

  • To delete this partition, press L.
     CAUTION: All data on this partition will be lost.

  • To return to the previous screen without
     deleting the partition, press ESC.

L=Delete ESC=Cancel

8   **7**

9

Windows XP Professional Setup

The following list shows the existing partitions and
unpartitioned space on this computer.

Use the UP and DOWN ARROW keys to select an item in the list.

  • To set up Windows XP on the selected item, press ENTER.

  • To create a partition in the unpartitioned space, press C.

  • To delete the selected partition, press D.

8057 MB Disk 0 at Id 0 on bus 0 on atapi [MBR]

    Unpartitioned space   8056 MB

117797 MB Disk 0 at Id 1 on bus 0 on atapi [MBR]

   E: Partition1 (DataDrive) [NTFS]   117797 MB (45550 MB free)

ENTER=Install C=Create Partition F3=Quit

10

Last chance

6 Windows gives you one more chance
to back out. This screen lists which
partition you have selected for
deletion, displaying its location,
partition type and size.

7 To return to the last screen press the
Esc key.

8 To delete the partition press the L key.

Select the space

9 Now you have removed the Windows
partition, Windows Setup gives you
the option of creating a partition in the
space left by the old partition.

10 You need to highlight the unpartitioned space, then press the C
key on the keyboard.

15

Preparing the disk ▶

Maximum size

1 Windows Setup will now ask you to choose a size for the new partition. A list of the minimum and maximum sizes is displayed.

2 In this case you want to choose the largest size available. Type in the number displayed in the maximum size section.

3 Press the Enter key to create the new partition.

Start the ball rolling

4 You now have a new unblemished partition. You can choose this and tell Windows setup to install XP onto it. Use the up and down arrow keys to select the new partition.

5 Press the Enter key to start the install.

For your information

You could choose a smaller size leaving space for another drive.

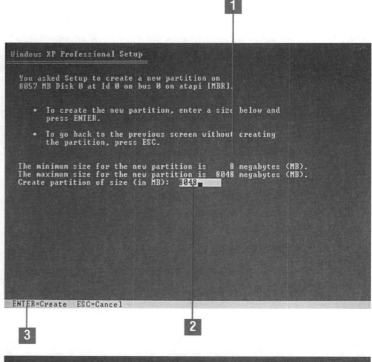

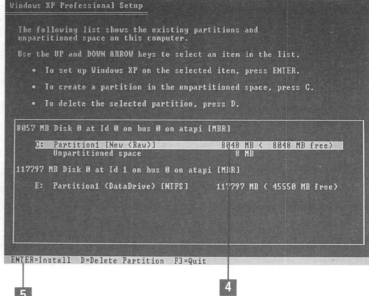

```
Windows XP Professional Setup

    The partition you selected is not formatted. Setup will now
    format the partition.

    Use the UP and DOWN ARROW keys to select the file system
    you want, and then press ENTER.

    If you want to select a different partition for Windows XP,
    press ESC.

        Format the partition using the NTFS file system (Quick)
        Format the partition using the FAT file system (Quick)
        Format the partition using the NTFS file system
        Format the partition using the FAT file system




   ENTER=Continue    ESC=Cancel
```

```
Windows XP Professional Setup




                        Insert the CD labeled:
                Windows XP Professional CD-ROM
                        into your CD-ROM drive.

                    • Press ENTER when ready.




   F3=Quit   ENTER=Continue
```

Which format to use?

6 As you have created a new partition, Setup needs to format it, so it can store files. You can select how the partition is formatted. Use the up and down arrows to highlight your choice.

7 Format NTFS quick formats the partition to the latest file system. It also does a quick format, which is considerably quicker than a normal format. For this task select this option.

8 Formatting the partition to the FAT32 file system ensures compatibility with older drives and systems.

New for old

9 When you create the partition you wipe out any traces of Windows XP. Windows will need to verify you have a have copy of Windows to upgrade from. This can be any previous version.

10 Remove the Windows install disk and temporally replace it with your previous full version of Windows. Close the CD-ROM drawer, wait a few seconds for the CD to mount then press the Enter key.

For your information

If you are using a full install Windows XP disk you will not see this message.

Loading Windows XP files

Informative

1 This screen is purely an information screen, which displays the progress of the format.

2 Windows will briefly check your hardware and then create a list of files that need to be copied to your computer so the setup can continue.

Copying begins

3 The Windows Setup program will now begin copying the installation files to your computer.

4 The progress bar gives you an indication of the percentage of the test completed.

5 This screen also tells you what files are being copied.

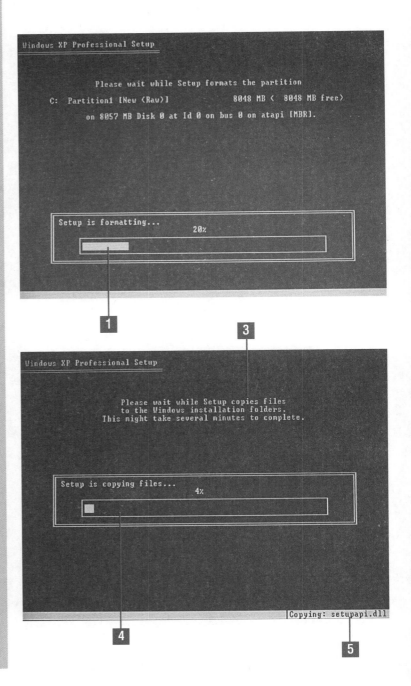

6

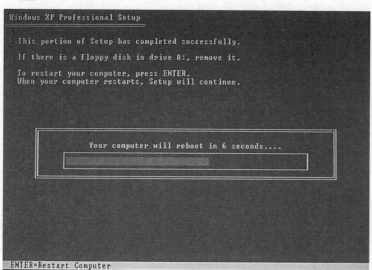

7

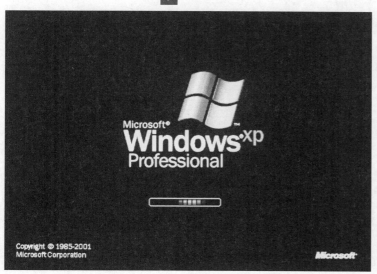

Let it get on with it

6 Copying the files to your computer can take a long time and you might want to leave your computer to get on with the job.

The first time

7 The Windows Splash screen is now displayed as Windows XP starts up for the first time to complete the installation.

15

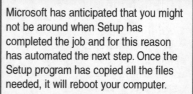

For your information

Microsoft has anticipated that you might not be around when Setup has completed the job and for this reason has automated the next step. Once the Setup program has copied all the files needed, it will reboot your computer.

Customizing
Windows XP

Finish up

1 The Windows Setup program will now work its way through the rest of the installation.

2 Setup lets you know how much longer the installation will take.

3 You can stay and read the snippets of information displayed on screen or nip off and make a cup of coffee.

4 When Windows Setup has finished copying all the files Setup will move on to configuration. Take the time to configure Windows XP at this point as it saves time once XP is installed. Click Customize.

5 You could click Next to accept the defaults, but you would be stuck with US settings. That means dollars instead of pounds and that's just the start.

Jargon buster

Default – the predefined choice for a setting which can be changed and has several options. This base choice is usually the one already in use and the safest option when troubleshooting.

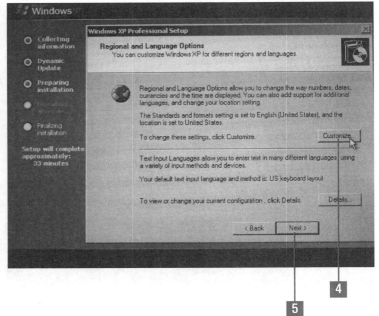

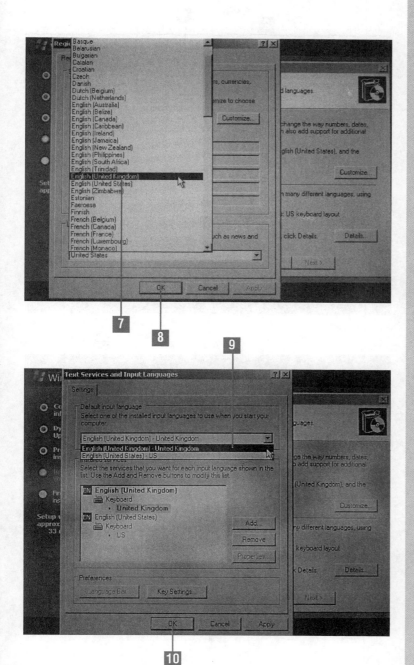

Regional settings

6 Click the down arrow next to the Country selection box.

7 A list of countries will be displayed, use the scroll bar to find English (United Kingdom), then click this option to select it.

8 Click OK to move on.

15

Keyboard setting

9 Repeat the process to select a country for the keyboard.

10 Click OK.

Customizing Windows XP (cont.)

Time after time

1 The Setup program will now ask you to select a time zone. Select GMT Greenwich Mean Time: Dublin, Edinburgh, Lisbon, and London.

2 This menu also lets you select the time and date. As this information was stored in your computer's CMOS chip this information should be correct.

3 When you have finished click Next.

Got the key?

4 The Windows Setup program will now ask you for your product key. Look on the back of the folder your Windows installation CD came in for a yellow sticker.

5 Type in the combination of letters and numbers shown on the sticker. The cursor will automatically jump from box to box once the correct amount of characters fill the box.

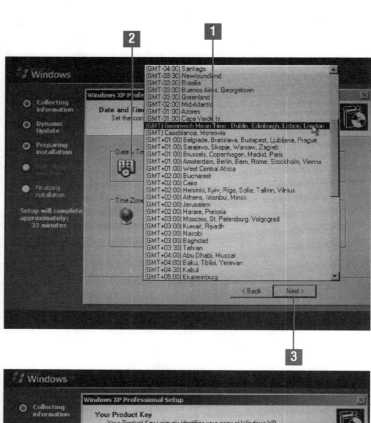

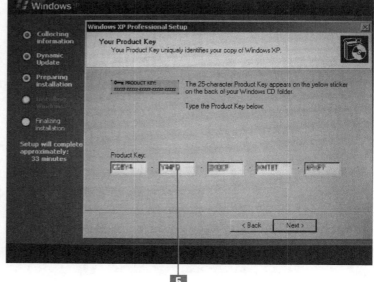

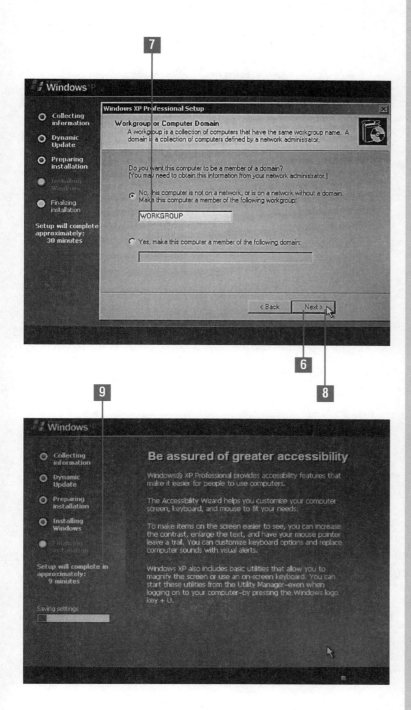

Customizing Windows XP (cont.)

Workgroup

6 Next a dialog box will ask you to setup a workgroup. If you are not planning to use your computer on a network just accept the default and click Next to continue.

7 If you are planning to use your computer on a network click into the box containing 'WORKGROUP'. Delete this and type in a description for your computer (for example, 'computer in bedroom' or 'John's computer').

8 When you are finished click Next to continue.

Last reboot

9 The Setup program will now save the settings you have just selected. When it's finished it will reboot the computer and the installation will be finished.

15

Using your common sense

Introduction

Computers can sometimes fool you into thinking that they are completely
lifeless. But before you panic there are a few simple checks you can carry out
to save you time and embarrassment.

Personal computers are highly modular by design. The most powerful troubleshooting technique is to isolate the problem to a specific component by trial-
and-error. Swap compatible components and see if the system still works. Try
different peripherals on different machines and see if the same problem
occurs. Make one change at a time.

Don't let them wear you down! Get stuck into computer problems. Try not to
see a broken computer as a problem – see it as an opportunity to learn more
about how your computer works. Troubleshooting can be part of the fun of
owning a computer. It can also be frustrating, but nothing beats the feeling of
knowing you solved the problem yourself!

Sometimes a problem just won't go away, you're only moments away from
cracking it, your solution should work and you have rebooted the PC for the
umpteenth time. Take a break; don't spend too long on the same problem. If
you feel like you want to throw the PC out of the window, it's time to leave it for
a while and do something completely different. You will be surprised how your
brain will often keep working on the problem without you really being aware of
it. When you do go back to it you will have some fresh ideas and new tactics
for tackling it. Finally, if you're really beat, call someone who can help. Make a
rule, never spend more than 2 hours on the same problem at any one time.

Always keep a record of what you have done. If you are upgrading or removing
kit make sure you note where things came from, which way up, etc. Is the red
cable to the right or the left? If you are troubleshooting a software problem
note all error messages. You may not know or need to know what they all
mean but if you have to resort to technical support they will need to know what
has happened. Many messages are self-explanatory and will point you in the
right direction, helping you get the problem solved quickly. You don't have to
copy the entire message onto a piece of paper. You can take a screen capture
much like the ones in this book. To do this simply press the PrintScrn button
on your keyboard. This will copy the screen. You can view the screen in a paint
package. Or copy them into your word processor and then print them out.

Checking connections

Many common computer problems can be traced back to cabling and connections. It is important to make sure all cables are in place and all plugs are connected firmly in their sockets. It not just the external cables that can give you trouble but also the internal cables such as the ones connecting your drives to the motherboard. These cables are called IDE and they are ribbon cables that can easily move when you install other equipment. Floppy drive cables also suffer the same tendencies. Even power cables can often work loose. Also, during transport, add-on cards such as graphics card and soundcards can pop out of their slots despite being screwed down.

Examine connections

1 There are many types of connections present in your computer's case. The first are the cables that connect via plugs to the motherboard. These are the main power supplier lead, switches and buttons.

2 Memory modules fit into slots or banks.

3 The main processor fits in the largest socket on the board.

4 Add-on cards such as sound and WiFi cards fit in free expansion slots.

5 The leads that supply power to individual devices.

6 Adaptors, which change the format of the plugs on the power supply leads for small sockets, for example, the sockets used on floppy drives.

Timesaver tip

When checking cables, a visual inspection is vital, but not always easy as other cables can get in the way. Gently ease the cables to one side being very careful not to dislodge any others and cause more problems.

Make sure all plugs and sockets are fully home. Look to see if the plug is fitting squarely and give it a push.

Try gently rocking the plug to the left and right as this will sometimes help to seat a plug fully in its socket.

DVD/CD-R drives are without doubt the cheapest and most reliable means of backing-up your hard drive, but sometimes even these can go wrong.

Erratic behaviour, such as system crashes (the horrible blue screen) and buffer under-runs, which inevitably result in a wasted disk, can be caused by a number of factors. The worst case is that your drive is faulty – but before you start reading it its last rites, try these remedies first.

Ensure that all the disks you put into the device are free of dirt and dust (a regular cause of the blue screen), and that the drive itself is clean. Buffer under-runs occur when your DVD/CD-R drive runs out of data to write and has to shut off its laser. Your computer must be fast enough to feed data uninterrupted to the drive, which means that you may have to reduce the write speed. Use the software's test-only option to find the optimum speed without causing errors or wasting a disk. Finally, you should ideally try to run no other applications when burning a CD-R.

Give me my CD-R

If your DVD/CD-R drive refuses to eject a disk, it could be for a number of reasons. It could be that the disk is still writing, in which case the eject mechanism is temporarily disabled. However, if it's finished, but still won't eject, it might be because the CD-R software has not re-enabled eject. Try right clicking on the drive icon on the Desktop and choosing 'Eject'. It might also be because the CD-R software has crashed, in which case you need to restart Windows.

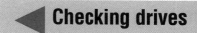

Checking drives

Eject a CD

1 Open the Start menu and select My Computer.

2 Once the My Computer menu is displayed you will see all the drives connected to your computer, including your DVD/CD-R drives.

3 Right-click on the icon that looks like a CD .

4 A pop-up menu is now displayed. Click Eject.

16

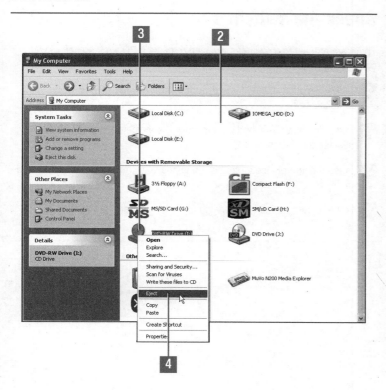

Checking the
obvious

Don't

If your machine freezes **do not**:

1 Press keys randomly.

2 Move the mouse rapidly.

3 Switch off immediately.

4 Hit the PC with something (though you may be tempted!).

5 Unplug and re-plug the keyboard, mouse or monitor.

Do

1 See if the mouse still moves the cursor. If it does wait for up to ten minutes.

2 Try Alt+Tab to switch to another application. If this works save your work and close the application.

3 Try Alt+Ctrl+Del to activate the Task Manager. End any tasks that might be blocking the machine.

If all of this fails then you will have to switch the machine off and on again.

Check the switches

There are at least four switches involved to make a PC work so before you conclude something is wrong check them all:

1 Is the computer plugged into a working socket with the electricity switched on?

2 Is the computer switched on – this may be indicated by a green light besides the switch.

3 Is the monitor plugged into a working socket with the electricity switched on?

4 Is the monitor switched on – again look for a green light to show it's working.

Timesaver tip

Never neglect the obvious! You will be surprised how often problems can have a very simple solution.

Error messages

17

Introduction

This list is **not** exhaustive or meant to resolve **every** error. It does, however, attempt to show examples of each type of error.

You are working away quite happily when, from nowhere, appears a little grey box full of gobbledegook giving you the general impression that all is not as it should be.

Eventually, every computer user will receive a cryptic note from Windows warning that some type of error has occurred inside their PC. Error messages in themselves are no bad thing, in essence they mean that a programmer has realised a problem has occurred and has had the foresight to warn you about it. Unfortunately, they did not have the foresight to write it in a language you could understand! Should, or rather when, an error message occurs, it is not uncommon for novices and experienced users alike to panic, but fear not! Whilst the white cross on the red background or the yellow exclamation mark can be intimidating there is often a fairly simple cure to the error they are indicating. Sometimes the user can be at fault and sometimes it can be the fault of the software or hardware – nobody's perfect and this is true of computers as well as humans. There are hundreds of different error messages you may see when you use Windows, although many of them will only appear in rare circumstances. It helps greatly if you can distinguish between the problems that you can solve and the problems that you can't. This chapter provides an 'identity parade' of common error messages with explanations of what they mean and what you can do to remedy them.

What you'll learn

Startup and system messages

Error messages about files

Other error messages

STOP errors

Troubleshooting STOP messages

Startup and system messages

Cannot find a device file . . .

This error message will appear in DOS when you are booting a machine up.

```
Cannot find a device file that may be needed to run windows or a windows application.

The windows registry or SYSTEM.INI file refers to this device file, but the device file no longer
exists.

If you deleted this file on purpose, try uninstalling the associated application using its uninstall
program or setup program.

If you still want to use the application associated with this device file, try reinstalling that
application to replace the missing file.

vnetsup.vxd
Press any key to continue
```

When you press a key as instructed, Windows may continue loading, and run normally.
Having to do this all the time soon gets pretty annoying; luckily we can tell you how to fix it.
This message occurs because a device driver, which Windows is instructed to load in one of
its configurations, has been deleted. Usually this is the result of deleting files manually, using
Explorer or My Computer instead of using the Add-Remove Programs facility. Think about any
software that you have recently removed from Windows and try reinstalling it. Have you or
anyone else been tinkering in the Windows folder recently? If you can remember which
program folder you moved it from try uninstalling and reinstalling the software/application. If
Windows runs normally without this file you can try removing the instruction to load it from
the configuration files. This, however, can be fairly tricky and we would advise against it
unless you really know what you're doing (or know someone who does!)

Invalid system disk

This message will appear in MS-DOS when your computer is
started. 'Pressing any key' will result in the same message
being displayed over and over. Despite the rather scary
sounding nature of this error message it is incredibly easy to
fix. When this message appears check your floppy drive and
you will find that you have left a floppy disk in it. This is the
non-system disk referred to by your computer. Remove it from
the drive, press any key and the computer will start as usual.

```
Invalid system disc
Replace the disk, and then press any key.
```

Startup and
system messages
(cont.)

Error reading CD-ROM

'Error Reading CD-ROM in Drive ...:'
'Please insert CD-ROM
With Serial Number ... in Drive ...:'

Interpretation – this usually means you have
attempted to eject a CD-ROM from the CD-ROM
drive while a program was accessing it. Sometimes
the error appears when the drive can't read a very
dirty, scratched, or otherwise damaged CD-ROM.
Either press the ESC key to close the error message
(and possibly crash the program that was accessing
the CD-ROM) or reinsert the CD-ROM and press
ENTER to attempt to let the program pick up where
it left off. Sometimes this error will freeze the
computer, and you'll have to use the Power or Reset
buttons on the front of your PC to get Windows'
attention. If a scratched or dirty CD-ROM caused the
error, clean the disk and try again, but frequently a
CD-ROM is damaged beyond repair if this message
shows up.

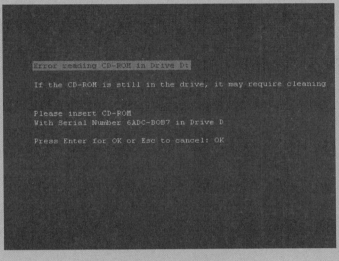

Since this message appears while the computer is booting, you won't have
to reset the machine to get into Safe Mode (a Windows mode that loads
minimal files to simplify troubleshooting). Just follow the error message's
prompts to load Windows, and a Registry Problem box will appear. Click the
Restore from Backup and Restart button and hope that the computer doesn't
experience any problems or power disruptions as Windows attempts to
restore the Registry from its automatically created archive of backup copies.
If the operation is successful, you can follow the prompts to reboot Windows,
and everything should be fine. If it doesn't work, you may have to reinstall
Windows, along with any hardware and software that was having trouble
when the Registry problem occurred.

Registry error?

'Warning: Windows has detected a Registry/
configuration error. Choose Safe mode to
start Windows with a minimal set of drivers'.
Interpretation – the Registry is a database
containing all the information Windows needs
to keep track of your hardware and software.
You should tend to this message immediately
because it is telling you there is a problem
with the all important Registry.

Jargon buster

Windows Registry – a database that
stores configuration data for Windows, for
both hardware and software. You can edit it
yourself using the RegEdit tool (start this
through the Run menu). You must be careful
as mistakes can cripple Windows.

Error messages about files

Hidden files

A fairly self-explanatory message this, but if you don't know what a hidden file is then you might get a bit stuck. Windows often hides files so that the user cannot easily tamper with them. Use the Select All command found under the edit menu in Explorer or My Computer and if there are hidden files present left click the mouse button on the Tools menu in the toolbar and then click on Folder options from the drop-down menu. From the dialog box click on the View Tab and finally the option Show All Files and click Apply to all files. You can also set Windows to always show hidden files by selecting Tools, Folder Options, View and clicking on Apply to all Folders. This works with any open Explorer window.

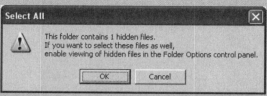

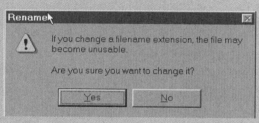

Filename extension

If you try to rename a file using Explorer and you are changing the file extension (the three letters that appear after the dot) then Windows will usually display this message. Be careful when changing file extensions, if you get it wrong then Windows won't know what program to use to open the file. If in doubt click No, so that Windows ignores the change.

Drag and drop error

In Windows XP you can drag and drop files. You can move the files or drag them onto a program so that you can open the file using the program you dragged the file onto. However, there are places you can't drag a file, like the taskbar and if you try to drag a file onto the taskbar Windows displays this Taskbar error message.

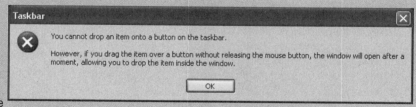

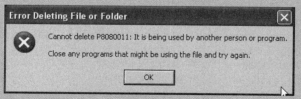

File in use

This is an example of Windows protecting itself or another file. If a file is being used by Windows or is open in another program, this implies the file is being worked on – Windows protects this file and will not let it be deleted until it is finished with and released.

Confirm File Replace?

'A file being copied is older than the file currently on your computer'. If this message appears in a grey box when you are installing some hardware or software, it means the application or hardware device driver software is attempting to overwrite a file already installed on your hard drive with an older version of that file. Always click yes to skip copying the file and keep the newer version. If the product you are installing doesn't work, make a backup copy of the newer version of the file, then try uninstalling and reinstalling the program, this time letting the older file overwrite the newer version. Usually programs run better when you leave the newer version alone.

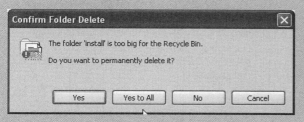

Recycle Bin warning

When deleting a large file this message will be displayed if the file can't fit in the Recycle Bin. If it won't fit into the Recycle Bin it won't be recoverable later. This warning box gives you the choice to permanently delete it or cancel the delete.

Source and destination

Easy mistake to make this, this message will appear if you try to copy a folder or a file to itself. Solution? Move it somewhere else!

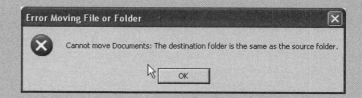

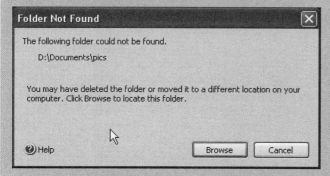

Folder Not Found

This error message will be displayed if you click on a shortcut which is set to a Folder location that no longer exists. You may have removed the folder and not the short cut.

Other error messages

Security Warning

This error is part of the improved Windows security system. It is a warning and is displayed if you or a rogue program attempts to download and run a program from the internet. If you are downloading a program then select save. If the message comes as a surprise cancel the operation.

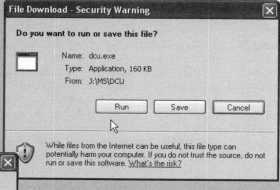

Microsoft now checks the digital signature of a software publisher before running a program that is run via the internet. If Windows does not recognise the publisher it will flag up a warning letting you decide if you want to run the program or not. It is not advisable to run a program without a valid digital signature.

Not formatted?

The drive referred to in this message is invariably the floppy drive. Although most disks are pre-formatted these days you may still come across this message. To format the disk just click on the button marked yes. If you are sure the disk has been used before, then check the disk in a different computer before you format it, as this will destroy all data on the disk.

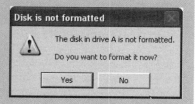

Speech bubble

Information speech bubbles appear bottom right hand side of the Windows desktop and hover above the taskbar. The job of these warnings is to keep you informed. They will inform you of changes and if any errors occurred while these changes were made.

Add or Remove error

This error is displayed if you use the Windows Add and Remove wizard to remove a program and Windows cannot find any uninstall information. This may be because the installer for the program did not follow Microsoft's rules for installers. It could be that the program has already been deleted without using Add and Remove. Or it could be that you are running Windows in Safe Mode.

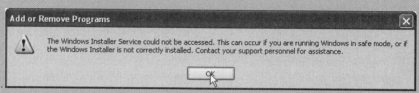

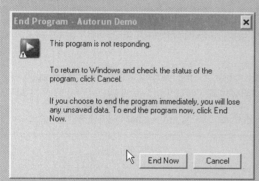

Program crash

Programs can and do crash, and when they do they stop talking to Windows. When this happens and Windows XP detects that a program is no longer responding, this message is displayed allowing you to end the program and carry on using Windows with no detrimental effects.

Internal Error?

'There was an internal error, and one of the windows you were using will be closed. It is recommended that you save your work, close all programs, and then restart your computer'. You most often see this when you open several windows from the same application. When one of the open window's experiences errors and crashes, this message pops up. Depending on the way the program is configured, sometimes this error closes only the offending window, and sometimes it brings down the entire program. Try to save whatever work you can before closing the error message. If only the error-producing window closes, shut down the program it was associated with before doing anything else (saving your work first, of course). Most of the time you can continue using your other open applications after you close the program that generated the error message, but it's usually better to heed the warning, save your work, and reboot.

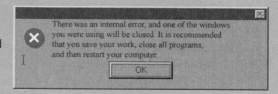

STOP errors

To test hard disk or volume integrity

1 In the Run dialog box, in the Open box type: cmd

2 Start the Chkdsk tool, which detects and attempts to resolve file system structural corruption. At the command prompt type:

chkdsk drive: /f

Jargon buster

FAT – File Allocation Table. How versions of Windows prior to XP organised storage on disk drives.

STOP messages mean just that. Windows has stopped! Most STOP messages are caused by hardware problems. An 8-digit hexadecimal number accompanies the message, for example a STOP 0x0000000A. An extra four additional 8-digit hexadecimal numbers may appear in parentheses and these would usually be unique to your hardware and the particular situation.

Common STOP messages

Stop 0x00000024 or NTFS_FILE_SYSTEM

The Stop 0x24 message indicates that a problem occurred within the NTFS.SYS file – this is the driver file that allows the system to read and write to NTFS file system drives. NTFS (new technology file system) is the way Windows XP organises files on disk. A similar Stop message, 0x23, exists for the FAT16 or FAT32 file systems.

Possible Resolutions:

1. Malfunctioning Small Computer System Interface (SCSI) and Advanced Technology Attachment (ATA) hardware or drivers can also adversely affect the system's ability to read and write to disk, causing errors. If using SCSI hard disks, check for cabling and termination problems between the SCSI controller and the disks. Periodically check Event Viewer for error messages related to SCSI or FASTFAT in the System log or Autochk in the Application log.

2. Verify that the tools you use to continually monitor your system, such as virus scanners, backup programs, or disk defragmenters are compatible with Windows XP. Some disks and adapters come packaged with diagnostic software that you can use to run hardware tests.

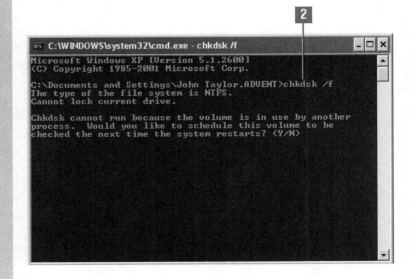

By running through the following checklist you stand a good chance of resolving the problems.

1. Examine the System and Application logs in the Event Viewer for other recent errors that might give further clues. To do this, launch EventVwr.msc from a Run box; or open Administrative Tools in the Control Panel then launch Event Viewer.

2. Have you added any new hardware? If so remove it and restart.

3. Use any hardware diagnostics supplied by the hardware manufacturer.

4. Are your device drivers and system BIOS up-to-date?

5. Conversely, if you've installed new drivers just before the problem appeared, try rolling them back to the older ones.

6. If you are confident, open your computer's case and make sure all hardware is correctly installed, well seated and solidly connected.

7. Check that all of your hardware is on the Microsoft hardware compatibility list. If some of it isn't, then pay particular attention to the non-HCL hardware in your troubleshooting.

8. Scan for any viruses.

9. Check any recently added software. Look on the software publishers sites for any known issues.

10. Examine, and try disabling, BIOS memory options such as caching or shadowing.

17

Technical support

Introduction

The internet holds a wealth of information – in fact it holds too much! Type troubleshooting in to any search engine and you will be bombarded with links – most of which are trying to sell you something. It takes many hours of research to find genuinely helpful sites. Even when you do find a site, what guarantee have you of the quality of information supplied? Well if you want to find out more about troubleshooting your PC then we have done the research for you and come up with some sites we recommend that not only help, but are technically sound. We have included some sites that are heavily forum-based. This is because these forums are a really effective way of getting an answer to your problem. Many users of forums are only too willing to help you, and you never know, you may be able to help out some of your future fellow forum users.

Who you'll visit

Computing.Net

HelpOnThe.Net: Tech Support Guy

PC Pitstop

Annoyances.org

Microsoft Windows XP Expert Zone Community

Techzonez

Computing.Net

Computing.Net, founded in February 1996, was built on the idea that no one technical support expert knows as much about solutions to problems as does the entire population of IT professionals. By using a forum-based message system, Computing.Net allows you to ask hundreds of technical support experts about your problem. Using the Computing.Net forums is simple and answers to questions are clear and easy understand. Computing.net says the forum has advantages over one-to-one technical support. As opposed to you having to email a technical support expert or chat with one directly, Computing.net forums allow previously answered questions to be found instantly, saving you and the support professional time. The forum system that Computing.Net uses has been rated as one of the best.

Computing.Net, however, is not only about forums. While the technical support forums are the backbone of Computing.Net, it also has many other forms of technical support, such as how-to's and instructions for beginners. By combining all of these services, Computing.Net contains all the information that a user is likely to need to receive technical support for his or her computer-related problems.

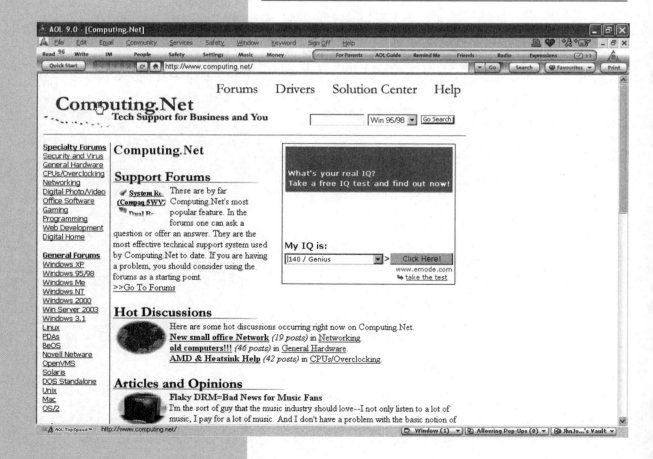

HelpOnThe.Net, founded in 1996, has been providing free technical support to computer users of all experience levels. Over 175,000 users have joined Tech Support Guy. This online support site is run completely by volunteers and paid for entirely by sponsors and donations from grateful members. That means it doesn't cost a thing for you to ask a question and this site believes there is no such thing as a stupid question so don't be afraid to ask. HelpOnThe.Net is divided into four great sections, including the Welcome Guide for new users and the Forums section that is run along similar lines to Computing.Net. There are always lots of other users who will help you – everyone is encouraged to muck in and help. The List server, designed as an alternative to the Forums, is an email list server, which allows you access to live user-to-user technical support via email.

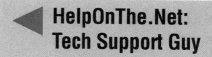

HelpOnThe.Net: Tech Support Guy

For your information

Tech Support Guy is at
http://www.helponthenet.com/

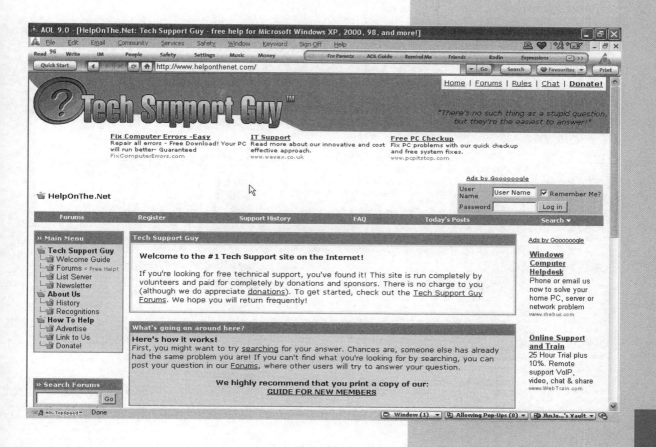

18

PC Pitstop

The PC Pitstop site mainly provides fix-it type software. However, they also have a free online forum, which has become one of the web's favourite watering holes for novices and gurus alike. This site provides valuable information, whether it's a Spyware clean-up or a performance tweak. Forums include User to User Help and Virus support. PC Pitstop forum regulars are helpful and will answer any question – once you have tried this site and its forums you will become a regular visitor.

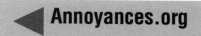
Annoyances.org

Annoyances.org is the most complete collection of information assembled for, and by users of, Microsoft Windows. This site is dedicated to stamping out annoyances. This site has many in-depth solutions in the form of articles that can be easily searched for via the sites search system. Annoyances.org covers a wide variety of Windows versions.

If you are new to Windows, or just new to Annoyances.org there is a Getting Started page which can be used as a launching pad to learn more about Microsoft Windows, and become familiar with Annoyances.org at the same time. There are also some great tips for beginners.

Where Annoyances.org excels is in its problem forums. If you are having a problem with Windows, or one of your applications, odds are someone else has experienced the same problem! The annoyances.org forum system allows you to search existing forum messages for messages related to your problem, or you can ask a question and get an answer from other Windows users.

For your information

Annoyances.org is at
http://annoyances.org/

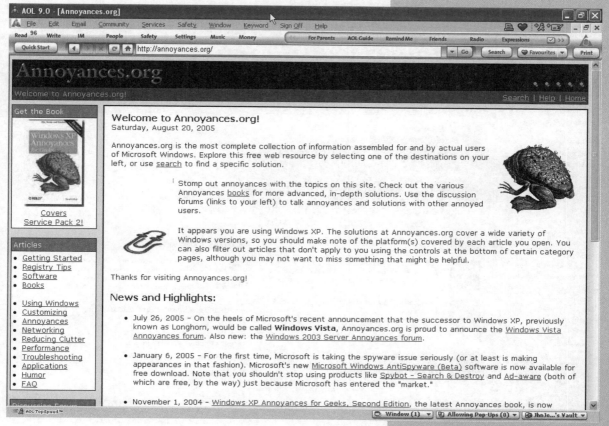

Microsoft Windows ▶ XP Expert Zone Community

Microsoft's official support forum is called The Microsoft Windows XP Expert Zone Community. It is an online community for Windows XP enthusiasts, and a leading resource where anyone can learn and gain expertise about the operating system.

Here you can contact people around the world who meet with and learn from each other online. Such online communities have proven to be especially valuable for exchanging information about support help. Microsoft has created a number of community websites, like the Expert Zone, to make it easy to learn from the knowledge and expertise of others online.

If you're not an expert yet, the Expert Zone is a great place to start. This is a vibrant online community and the more people who join in the better it gets. Microsoft say don't be shy, ask questions and learn.

For your information

Microsoft Windows XP Expert Zone Community is at

http://www.microsoft.com/windowsxp/expertzone/default.mspx

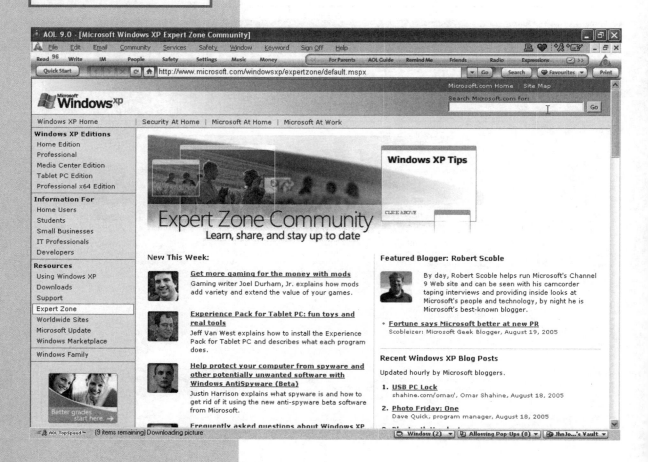

The Techzonez site is a forum site, which aims to keep you up-to-date with news and events. All the forums are fully searchable and users are encouraged to get involved.

Discussions are organised into threads, which gather together all the posts from users on a subject. You can start your own thread or become involved in an existing one. You can search for posts based on username, word(s) in the post or just in the subject, by date, or in particular forums. To access the search feature, click on the Search link at the top of most pages. You can search any forum that you have permission to search – you will not be allowed to search through private forums unless the administrator has given you the necessary security rights to do so.

Techzonez

For your information

Techzonez is at
http://www.techzonez.com

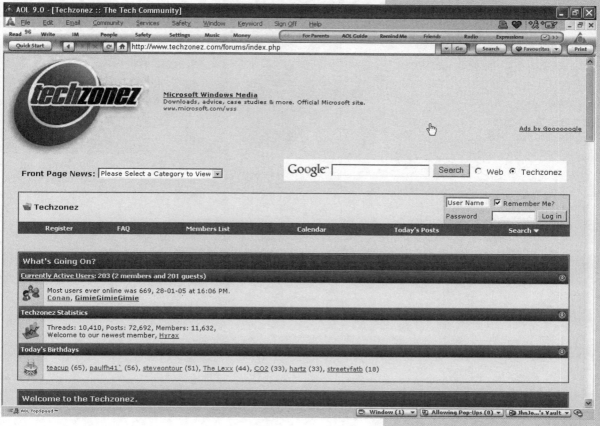

18

Jargon buster

Adware – installed along with other applications and delivers adverts, sometimes through the application window and sometimes through pop-up windows. Often Adware is more of an annoyance than a genuine threat, as many free programs use it to bring in money.

AGP – an Accelerated Graphics Port is a high speed connection for video cards. On most motherboards there is only one of them and older computers do not have AGP. AGP is faster than PCI and has direct access to system memory so that the computer's memory it is therefore better for 3D graphics and games.

Application – an executable program capable of performing a specialized function, other than system maintenance (which is performed by utilities). Games, educational programs, and communications software are all examples, as are word processors, spreadsheets and databases.

Archive – a collection of files and often a zip file is referred to as an archive or compressed archive.

Auto-update – software that auto-updates will download and install the latest version of itself, often without user-intervention. Sometimes called a live update.

Backup – a single file containing data that might normally be stored in many files or folders. It is created to safeguard against future data loss due to system failure or overwriting of data.

BIOS – Basic Input/Output System can be found on your computer's motherboard. It controls the most basic operations and is responsible for starting your computer up and checking all hardware attached to the computer.

Boot – switch on and start up the computer and its operating system.

Broadband – traditionally the name given to a service which uses a single wire to carry many signals, for example cable telephone services that also provide television. Recently it has been applied to fast internet connections though ISPs will call anything from 256k upwards broadband when many don't believe that is true broadband as it's not fast enough. Most broadband connections now are at least 512k.

Buffer – a temporary storage area in memory that contains data that's being transferred from one place to another. For example; when you are making a CDROM disk using files stored on your hard drive, the buffer acts as a go-between to ensure that data is flowing smoothly to the CD-R drive. If the data runs out the disk write won't wait for it and the write will fail. Buffer under-run protection stops this happening.

Bug – a malfunction due to an error in the software or a defect in the hardware. Programs don't work as they should, become erratic or stop working.

Command prompt – an even more restricted version of Windows than Safe Mode with no graphics support, which only allows you to type in commands.

Cookie – a file sent to your computer by a website. A cookie is meant to contain non-sensitive data (not credit card details or log-in passwords) about who you are. This enables the site to be customised just for you. For example, lots of sites use cookies to recognise you when you log-on, and show a personalised greeting. Cookies can track how you use the internet.

Computer administrator – when applied to user accounts, the administrator account means that person has full access to the entire system, including the ability to install and remove software and other tasks affecting the administration of the system. When we're talking about networks and corporate computer systems, the admin is the person in charge of maintaining the systems.

Context menu – the term given to the menu that appears when you right-click, so called because its functions change depending on the program or area of the operating system in which you currently reside.

Control Panel – an important area of Windows that contains links to settings and controls for hardware, software and peripherals.

Default – the predefined choice for a setting which can be changed and has several options. This base choice is usually the one already in use and the safest option when troubleshooting.

Defrag – (defragment). Fragmentation is where files are split into multiple parts around a hard disk. When you defrag, the file system joins these fragmented parts back together, or at least moves them closer to each other, so that the hard disk has less work to do when searching.

Dialog box – Windows uses these boxes to display a message on the screen, or the choices that a program provides. It often contains buttons, check boxes, radio buttons, and text boxes.

Directory (often referred to as folder) – a way of organising a collection of files on your computer's hard drive or other media into separate compartments, much in the same way as drawers in a filing cabinet. The main directory is called the root directory, with all the other sub-directories stemming from it. You can organise files in a directory in many ways, such as alphabetically, or by type, size or date.

Disk – exist in four distinct types: the 'hard' disk that is inside the computer and stores vast amounts of data. The 'floppy' disk which is portable, 3.5" square, and can store about 1.4 megabytes of data. The 'optical' disk which encompasses CDROM, CDR, CDRW, DVD, DVDRW, DVD-R DVD-RW and specialised types. 'Zip' disks, which are like floppy disks but can hold more data.

Disk cache – with reference to hard drives, this is a designated folder where your computer stores files for later use, such as the Temporary Internet Files folder for Internet Explorer. This enables the computer to find and retrieve them faster than it could otherwise. Disk caches are also used to read-ahead data, where they predict the next lot of information to be read on the hard drive, again making access to files that much faster.

Disk drive – the equipment that holds the (fixed or removeable) disk, and stores on or retrieves information from it.

DMA (Direct Memory Access) – a way of sending information from a storage device directly to the memory without passing the information through the processor.

DPI (Dots Per Inch) – a measure of the quality of the printed output. A small number is associated with budget printers; high quality photo-realistic printers offer higher DPI settings.

DOS – the software underneath all versions of Windows prior to Windows XP. It uses a text-based command line to control the computer. Short for Disk Operating System, this is the command line interface part of your PC, and is used to control basic input and output operations and other processor functions, as well as to control peripherals. Most software (even games) now run under Windows, and depending on which version of Windows you have DOS is either hidden or no longer used and so the need to know how to use it is becoming less important.

Download – the act of transferring a file from a remote computer connected to the internet or network to your own computer.

Driver – a small program that enables add-on accessories to talk to your computer. Without the appropriate driver software installed, Windows cannot transmit to or receive from a device, whether it's a printer, CD-ROM drive or scanner.

DVD (digital versatile disks) – CD-ROM-like disks that can store large amounts of data in digital form – 133 minutes of high-resolution, wide-screen video or 4.7 gigabytes (GB) of data. These disks are replacing CD-ROMs as well as VHS videotape and laser disks.

Encryption – the conversion of data into a scrambled code, so that it cannot be read by normal means. Encrypted data must be unscrambled before it can be accessed. Most encryption is not completely foolproof but modern encryption techniques take a large amount of skill and computing power to crack.

EXE – a file with the .EXE extension means that it is an executable program file, a self-contained program that will run on its own. This can be a software installation package or application.

Extension – the letters after a filename that tell you what kind of data the file contains. For example '.jpg' is a JPEG image and '.txt' is a text file.

FAT32 (File Allocation Table 32) – the 32-bit file system available since Windows 95, which supports hard disks of up to 2 terabytes in size.

File – a collection of computer data that has been saved with a single name and usually a file extension to identify its type. It could be text, music, a photo, part or a whole program or many other types of data.

File extension – indicates to you and the operating system the type of file. The response when the file is opened varies depending on the application with which it is associated. Windows will prompt the user to select an action when unrecognised files are accessed.

Firewall – a barrier between the internet and your computer. It protects from outside threats like viruses and hackers by filtering the incoming data, blocking any potentially harmful information. Firewalls are an absolutely vital part of any system connected to the internet.

Firmware – the built-in controller software, which resides on a programmable chip within a hardware device. Since this chip is re-programmable, it may be upgraded through a firmware patch. Updating firmware goes some way to future-proofing devices and allows you to share developments and improvements that occurred after the manufacture of the device.

Floppy drive – or FDD, is used to read 3.5" magnetic media. These disks hold just 1.44 MB so are quickly becoming outdated. Older floppy drives used 5.25" disks.

Folders – what Windows uses to organise all the files. Think of them like the filing cabinets in an office, a way of keeping relevant files grouped together for easy access. See also *directories*.

Freeware – software available at no cost to the user. Often freeware is distributed through the internet or dial-up modem connections.

Formatting – the process of preparing a disk to receive data.

Graphics card – provides specialised graphics acceleration, allowing for advanced visuals and effects. Using a dedicated card rather than an onboard graphics solution takes pressure off the CPU.

Hard disk drive – the primary storage medium for PCs. They are a non-volatile type of memory.

Heatsink – used to transfer heat away from components and are often used in conjunction with fans. They're required for CPUs and most modern graphics cards, which run at extremely high temperatures.

Hot keys – the popularity of the internet has brought about new keyboards with extra buttons, known as hot keys. These hot keys usually allow you to jump to your email or favourite website by pressing a single button. You'll need to make sure you've installed the software that came with your keyboard if you want these hot keys to work.

Icons – on-screen symbols or pictures that relate to program files or other computer functions. Clicking on an icon will start an action, e.g. open a file or run a program. The picture will usually give a clue as to what the program does or which program a file is used with.

IDE (Integrated Drive Electronics) – standard interface protocol for hard disks. The disk controller is an integrated part of the hard disk unit. This standard is now being superseded by a new standard called SATA.

Input – data that is entered into a computer. This can be words, pictures, sound, or simple control information. Input can come from keyboards, mice, scanners and the internet etc.

Interface – two types: software and hardware. A software interface is a program front end which is displayed on screen so that a user can interact with it. Hardware interfaces are the physical connections.

IRQ (Interrupt Request) – signals, which tell the CPU to halt its current task and await further instructions. Different computer components, such as modems, keyboards, mice, sound cards and other devices each have a special IRQ set aside for them to use. If a newly added piece of hardware tries to use the same IRQ as an existing device on older computers this would lead to conflict and one or both of the devices will not function properly. Windows XP and Plug and Play now deal with these problems.

Jumper – a circuit bridge that allows the user to adjust the settings of a device by covering the jumper pins with a plastic plug.

LED (Light Emitting Diode) – a small light that shows that the power is on.

LAN (Local Area Network) – a way of linking computers to share files and resources such as printers. Wireless networks are becoming common in offices and homes.

License agreement – the legalese that appears whenever you install software and lays out exactly what you can and can't do with an application. For the average home user there's probably not much of relevance or interest, if you're planning on using a program in a business capacity however you might want to have a read as some free applications require business users to purchase a license.

Live updates – allow a program to download new versions of itself or, in the case of spyware and antivirus tools, new information about threats to keep your system protected. Generally, live updates should be done in the background without requiring any user intervention.

Local printer – the one attached to your computer as opposed to a printer located elsewhere in the building or on someone else's computer.

LPT1 – the standard printer socket on the back of the computer is a unique shape and design so that only the printer lead will fit it. It is possible, though unusual, to have two or more and these will be called LPT2 and so on. The USB port has now superseded this socket.

Malware – a catch-all term for software installed by stealth onto a PC for malevolent purposes (hence the name).

Memory – areas which the computer's main processor uses to store, manipulate and run programs. The amount of memory a computer has is measured in megabytes or gigabytes. The more you have the more you can do.

Menu – a list of choices in a program. Menus can take many forms, from a simple windows list, a pull-down list under a heading in a menu bar or a collection of icons.

Monitor – the TV-like display connected to the main PC unit.

Motherboard – like the central nervous system of your PC, the other components all connect to the motherboard which then shunts data to the correct location.

MP3 – a file format for music, MP3 is a compression standard, which reduces the file size of a music file. This compression is achieved by removing sound outside the spectrum humans can hear. MP3 files have become the way of sharing music over the internet.

Numeric keypad – the number keys to the right of the main keyboard.

Optical drive – used to read and write to CDs and DVDs. All new DVD drives can read and write both CDs and DVDs. Older drives may be read-only or capable of handling a particular type of DVD.

Parallel port – the printer or LPT port. The names comes from the fact that print data is sent down several wires simultaneously and the signals travel parallel to each other.

Partition – a method of dividing a hard drive into multiple virtual drives.

Patch – software updates that fix holes or introduce new features into a program.

PCI (Peripheral Component Interconnect) – a personal computer local bus designed by Intel – PCI compatible add-on cards plug into a PCI slot on the motherboard.

PCI-Express – the 'sequel' to PCI and AGP interfaces, PCI-express offers a (potentially) huge increase in bandwidth. Newer motherboards include one or two PCI-e slots specifically for graphics cards and several more for additional expansion cards, alongside a couple of standard PCI slots.

A **peripheral** is something not core to your computer; this usually means an add-on like a web-cam or speakers. Most peripherals are extra things you buy to add to the functionality of your computer such as a printer or scanner.

Personal computer (PC) – originally referred to as IBM compatible computers, one that conformed to the standards set down by IBM for format, make up and which software it used.

Photorealistic – a term used for a printer that is capable of outputting photographs that look like they have been developed and printed in the traditional way.

Pixel – derived from picture element. It refers to the individual dots that, when grouped, make up a video display's picture or a digital camera's image-capture area. If you look very closely at your monitor, you can see its pixels.

Plug and Play – a system that allows you to add devices and accessories to your computer without configuring either the device or computer. This ensures all devices work as soon as they are plugged in and all devices work with each other.

POST (Power On Self-Test) – the check that every computer runs when it first powers up, to ensure that all necessary hardware is present and correct.

Power supply – a small metal box inside the computer that takes main voltage in and converts it to the lower voltages that the computer needs to operate, often abbreviated to PSU.

Printer port – a large socket at the back of the computer to which a printer can be attached. The same as a parallel port or LPT. Most printers now use USB ports so this socket is no longer used to connect newer printers.

A **process** is a small program that contains the control information necessary for the execution of a program. If you have an internet connection, firewall and virus protection, the list of processes can be a lengthy one.

PWL file – a file in the Windows folder that contains all the Microsoft passwords used by your machine.

RAID (Redundant Array of Independent Disks) – is a way of storing the same data in different places on multiple hard disks. This preserves the data if one drive goes down.

RAM (Random Access Memory) – provides temporary storage for files that are in use. RAM is volatile memory and loses the data held when power is switched. Windows and other software require large amounts of RAM to operate.

Recycle Bin – a folder linked to an icon on the Windows Desktop where you can drag folders or files that you want to delete. When you put items into the Recycle Bin, they are not permanently deleted, and can be easily recovered by double-clicking on the Bin icon, and restoring them back to their original folders. To permanently delete a file, you need to empty the Recycle Bin.

Registry – see *Windows Registry*.

Rescue disk – provides help in a computer emergency by booting up your system with a variety of diagnostic tools. Many programs offer the ability to create rescue disks, some of which allow you to scan for and clean viruses or restore your computer to a previous state.

Resolution – defines the clarity of an image. With monitors, the resolution describes the number of pixels on screen, so a 1280x1024 resolution means that there are 1024 lines of 1280, a total of 1,310720 pixels. The maximum resolution changes depending on the capabilities of the monitor. All new 17-19" LCD monitors are capable of anything up to 1280x1024, with larger monitors handling 1600x1200 and varying specifications for widescreen displays.

Safe Mode – a minimal operating version of Windows, which should always work unless there are serious hardware problems.

SATA (Serial Advanced Technology Attachment) – an interface for connecting hard drives to your computer. SATA uses serial signalling technology. Because of this the SATA cables are thinner than the ribbon cables used by IDE hard drives.

Sector – division of a disk. Sectors are grouped into tracks. The boot sector of a disk is the first sector, and is used to start the operating system.

Shareware – copyrighted software distributed on a pay-if-you-like and keep basis. Some software has built-in time limits and some relies on honesty.

Shell – a software interface between you and your computer's operating system. The shell interprets commands entered by the user, and passes them on to the operating system. The DOS command line is an example of a shell.

Shortcut – link to another location on your computer. If you want to run an application, they save you from navigating to the directory where that program is stored.

Spyware – applications that monitor your computer and return data about your activities to the people or person's who created them. Often combined with adware. Many spyware applications are malicious, intrusive and incredibly stubborn, proving extremely difficult to remove once they're into your system. In many cases, there's a thin line between spyware and virus.

Start Menu – appears when you click the Start button on the Windows taskbar. It's a vital part of Windows, containing links to applications and various parts of the operating system such as the Control Panel.

Substitution test – a simple way of checking that part of a computer works by swapping it for an equivalent part from another computer that can reasonably be assumed to be working.

SVGA (Super VGA) – a display standard. The generally accepted definition is 800 x 600 with a minimum of 256 colors at that resolution.

System Tray – the little box on the right-hand side of the Taskbar in Windows. As well as displaying the time and date, it is a place where you can quickly launch various system configuration tools, such as the Volume control and, if you have one installed, a Virus scanner. The System Tray is also used to display the status of certain Windows functions, such as when you're connected to the internet.

Swap file – a file placed on the computer's hard drive and used by Window as virtual memory. Information that is in the computer physical memory but not being used is copied into this file until it's needed again. When needed, the data is swapped back into physical memory, trading places with other infrequently needed parts. This stops you running out of memory – however swap files are the reason some PCs run slowly.

Taskbar – the bar at the bottom of the display in Windows that stretches from one side of the display to the other. Program icons are shown here allowing you to access any application running by clicking it on the taskbar.

TCP/IP (Transmission Control Protocol/Internet Protocol) – the basic communication language or protocol of the internet. It can also be used as a communications protocol in a LAN.

Toolbars – groups of related options and tools, usually represented by icons. Toolbars can be floating in a program window or embedded into the top or side of an application window (sometimes called sidebars.) Sidebars are often customisable, giving users the option to disable them or add and remove icons.

Trojan – just about the worst type of malicious program, because its sole purpose is to deliver a package. They can masquerade in many forms, but are commonly created within another fully functional program. When you are running a new third-party software package and your firewall asks you questions regarding permission for internet or network traffic, the chances are high that a Trojan is to blame.

Upload – the process of transferring one or more files from your computer to one on the internet. Some scanners expect you to upload a file to check it.

USB (Universal Serial Bus) – a type of connection (plug and socket) used to attach external add-ons to your computer. Up to 127 USB devices can be daisy-chained to one port. You can plug and unplug these accessories while the computer is switched on. USB ports can usually be found at the back of the computer but can also be found at the front in better-designed computers, and can be present in an external hub.

VGA (Video Graphics Array) – an IBM-defined standard resolution of 640 x 480 with 16 colors.

Virus – a program that has been deliberately created to cause problems on your computer. Though usually minor they can erase your entire hard disk. Viruses are commonly spread via email as an attachment or by removable storage media (floppies, CDs, etc.). Never open an attachment you are unsure of!

Virtual memory – the name given to the process of using an area of the hard drive as substitute real memory. When your computer is running low on physical memory, it temporarily copies parts of the real RAM to the hard disk, enabling you to open larger documents and more programs than physical memory allows.

WAN (Wide Area Network) – a way of connecting computers over a long distance not just within a home or office. The internet is an example of a very big WAN.

WiFi (wireless fidelity) – a standard protocol for wireless local area network (WLAN) IEE 802.X

Wildcards – a symbol used to represent one or more other symbols. Windows generally accepts two wildcards: the asterisk (*) and the question mark (?). The asterisk is used in place of any alphanumeric combination. And the question mark is used to represent a single alphanumeric character.

Windows Registry – a database that stores configuration data for Windows, for both hardware and software. You can edit the registry yourself using the RegEdit tool, which is accessed through the Run menu. You must be careful though as mistakes can cripple Windows.

Wizard – a special program that provides a step-by-step guide to performing a task, such as installing a printer. It tells you what to do and prompts you to enter any information it requires.

Worm – a malicious program that uses network communications to spread to multiple computers. Worms commonly use your email service and send themselves to email addresses within your contacts and other email folders. For this reason, always keep an eye on your sent items folder, and try putting a spoof address at the beginning of your contacts list.

Zip – This is a collection of files that have been highly compressed to save space and speed up downloading from the internet. You need a zip utility like WinZip or Winrar to extract the files from the archive.

Zip drive – This is a special disk drive that uses high capacity disks of 100 or 250Mb. They are like thick floppies. A Zip Drive can be attached to the parallel printer port or SCSI interface and so has the potential to cause problems with some printers, although most now connect through USB.

Troubleshooting guide

Index

T

U

V

W